HEAL YOURSELF

Full Guide to Energy

By: Jennifer Scordamaglia

Heal Yourself: Full Guide to Energy...

Copyright © 2026 by Jennifer Scordamaglia - All rights reserved. First Edition

No part of this book may be reproduced, stored in a retrieval system, or transmitted in any form or by any means—electronic, mechanical, photocopying, recording, or otherwise—without the prior written permission of the author, except for brief quotations in critical reviews or articles.

Disclaimer: The information in this book is for educational and informational purposes only based on personal experience. It is not intended as a substitute for professional medical advice, diagnosis, or treatment. Always seek the advice of your physician or other qualified health provider with any questions you may have regarding a medical condition. The author and publisher disclaim any liability for any loss or damage incurred as a result of the use or application of any of the contents of this book.
For inquiries: info@spreadpositivenergy.com

Library of Congress Control Number: 2025927276

ISBN: 979-8-9943583-9-9

To my dedicated collective of twenty-seven nomadic meditators, my husband, and the late Dr. Don Pedro Joaquín Valencia— all whose wisdom and guidance ignited this journey.

And to all seekers of truth and inner light, may these pages awaken your true potential and heal the world within.

Table of Contents

Introduction	9
Life	13
Understanding what we are	21
Birth	27
Puberty	35
The tree of life	49
Mental Programming	53
Guided by the universe	68
Emotions	77
Self-Love	87
Beauty	93
Negativity	97
Positivity	109
Karma	117
Angels & Demons	121
Understanding Energy	131
Wasting Energy	141
Friends	151
Relationships	155
The Shield	165
Meditation	177
Intuition	185
Open Channel	189
Transcending	195
Sexual Minds	201
Sexual Energy	207

Our Conduit	213
The Yoni	219
The Lingam	223
Soft vs Hard	243
Orgasm	249
Pleasure	255
What level are you in?	269
Desire	275
Chemical Imbalance	281
Female recovery	287
Awakening Sensitive spots	293
Using Energy for Health, Wealth & Love	299
Energy Retention	305
Love vs Lust	313
Perseverance	317

Introduction: My Journey to Unlocking True Energy

For the past seventeen years, I've been on an extraordinary path, guided by a dedicated collective: twenty-seven nomadic meditators, my husband, and the late Dr. Don Pedro Joaquín Valencia—a pioneering medical doctor, sexologist, and investigator who spent his final sixteen years in retirement studying me and others. Together, we bridged science and sexual energy, pinpointing the hidden roots of health issues tied to our intimate patterns and discovering profound healing through energy practices. In 2009, I made a bold choice: granting those twenty-seven meditators unrestricted, 24/7 access to my mind. Their mission? To hear my every thought, every emotion, feel my bodies progress, heal and reignite the innate gift of energy they sensed was being hijacked by negativity. Every insight in this book—channeled, meditated upon, rigorously tested, and proven—comes from our group of thirty souls. We've distilled what truly works from what doesn't, leading to transformative shifts in my body, my life, and the lives of countless others. While some concepts here may echo universal truths found elsewhere, I've never drawn from outside sources. My knowledge is pure, born from our meditations and direct experiences—unfiltered by books, gurus, or trends. I've lived every trial and error, ensuring authenticity in what I share. Why? Because true wisdom demands personal embodiment. We'll embark on a step-by-step journey: exploring the essence of energy, how your mind operates amid invisible forces, and practical ways to harness it for everyday resilience, success, and fulfillment on all levels—physical, emotional, and spiritual. Then, midway through, we dive into the heart of it: sexual energy. Seventeen years ago, sex felt to me like it does to most— an overwhelming, mysterious force, often misunderstood and mishandled. But uncovering the body's true mechanics unleashes a Pandora's box of revelations, shattering illusions about what's "normal" or "inevitable." From my own starting point—a 100% blocked channel drowned in negativity—to a 99% open flow of positivity, I've navigated the pitfalls: overcoming damaging habits, healing without conventional medicine, and witnessing the stark contrast between misuse (which sabotages health and vitality) and mastery (which ignites ecstasy, renewal, and awakening).In my own raw words, I'll guide you through these discoveries, empowering you to make wiser choices and tap into humanity's untapped potential. This isn't just my story—it's a blueprint for future generations. A word of caution: Some truths here may challenge your beliefs, stir discomfort, or evoke regret. Embrace them. Openness is the key to growth. Living blindly serves no one; together, we can shift the world's energy toward light and healing. Are you ready to begin?

Life

It is important for you to look at your life from a different perspective, as if it weren't your own, so that you can analyze your parents from a third-party perspective. Being lenient and understanding, forgiving because they only taught us what they were taught and what they felt was right for us at that time. Some people do not receive love in their youth simply because those raising them never felt what love was, so if we were to think about it, we must go back into a lot of previous generations, from grandparents to great-grandparents, and further on to really understand how and why our education at home was the way it was. Our ancestors and family traumas, even those that we have never heard of before, and we'll never find out about, are with us in our lineage and genes. It is up to us to decode everything that we live through today in our current life and identify which of those characteristics belong to us or belong to someone in our lineage that we must detach from and heal for them so that this vicious cycle of family traumas finally finds an end at some generation. Maybe you come from a loving family where everything was perfectly put for you and explained, and you were well educated at all levels, and nothing bad ever happened to you. Maybe you come from a family where your parents work too much, and they didn't have enough time to raise you.

You jumped around from family to family, or foster homes, or very negative lifestyles, and you were never really surrounded by any love, affection, or good examples. So, I would like to begin this journey of ours by acknowledging our roots, who and where we come from, the teachings that we received, and the lack of teachings we might have missed out on. Following up with the thought of: did we receive enough amount of love when we were growing up, did we feel like we had a companion when we most needed it, did we feel supported, did we feel safe? All of this will have an important impact on the character and person we are today. So, if we want to open our minds to new possibilities of a better life, the first thing we must do is understand without justification, accept, and forgive those who had a large impact on our foundation as children. Because if you do not come from a place of warmth and positivity, your best reset is to try to put into perspective why whoever raised you was the way they were, what trauma made them act in certain ways, and forgive their soul. This will disconnect the pain. Some people say they will never forgive. No matter how horrible and how right you might be, the only person you are hurting by not forgiving yourself is yourself. You forgive yourself to heal, to allow yourself to let go of that pain. If you do not welcome this change and aren't open to a new beginning, then it will never happen on its own.

If you have never had an example of love, you are never going to know how to give love, but you are most definitely still with the opportunity to learn.

We exist in a time in society where the energetical culture, family-based and foundation are totally broken. A system is built to create cracks in the stability of a family, where parents barely have time for themselves and their kids. People expect institutions to bring valuable teachings to their home when all they care about is to have another sheep in the herd they can manipulate and benefit from. Freedom comes in many ways, but the most important ones are the ones you can't see. How free is your mind, spirit, and energy? How much time do you really take on your spiritual growth, on your well-being, and on your true happiness? How much time do you spend trying to be someone accepted by society's norms, where you do not question or doubt anything that's said to you, because all you care about is being accepted? We are not meant to fit in. If you are trying to fit into a society whose world is broken, you are breaking yourself as well. We are meant to stand out and enlighten as many people as we can with our awakening. But first, you must awaken.

I hope that further on in this reading, you will find some clarity in the path you're looking for, where I will do my best to transmit my personal experience of energy and personal growth to those of you who are seeking to connect back to your true self. Now that your mind is open...

To understand what we are, we first must open our minds to the concept of us as infinite. We come from infinite, and we are a part of it in small particles. Take a deep breath through your nose, hold it for 3 seconds and blow it out pushing air out of your mouth, then close your eyes for 10 seconds thinking this: imagine a space where everything is white around you surrounded by brightness, the feeling of weightless and a profound serenity and lightness where there is no worries, no time, no thoughts, just existence and fulfillment.

We all remember where we come from; it is just sunk deep in our subconscious, buried under ideologies, customs, and culture. We are born with a wiped hard drive for our journey to be unique again, that's the idea, but we can access our prior lifetimes if that's what we want. What if, from the moment our brains activated, our absorption of reality was so different? What if we were never taught a religion, or cultural manners, or even a language? Would it matter? Would we have no other way of communicating? Our soul is the most valuable possession in the galaxy; it's an infinite power source, and the body we carry is a vessel that needs to be exercised for this power source to flourish.

We come from a place called Ether. Science, as slow as it is regarding energy and spiritual topics, has for once proven that when our soul leaves our body, our physical body is an ounce lighter and our soul travels to what they have discovered to be another galaxy, which they already named, but it's the Ether. This is the place where time and space do not exist; it's a space of fulfillment, it's a space of lightness, it's a space of wholesomeness, it's a space of hope and positivity, and it's a space where you see things a lot differently than our physical realm, without prejudice, ideologies, or norms. What gives us the sense of needing to judge what's happening around us is 100% influenced and affected by ideologies that have been taught to us since the moment we arrived on this planet. So, if we were to remove our arrival to this physical realm and we solely base our perception on our energy and the energy of others, we would probably not think the way that we do in our everyday life. We are born light; the moment we arrive on this earth; our light has to be protected and fed from the energy of our parents or those who raise us. If, for whatever reason, we are deprived of that protection, we are vulnerable to absorbing negative energies around us, because, in case you did not know, there is a never-ending battle in the universe between positive and negative. Just like the show you in the movies. You are not aware of it because you are living your life. But when you integrate yourself into being a light worker, you are exposed to seeing other realities and dimensions, which make life so much more interesting. So, the moment there's pureness somewhere on this planet, negativity will always try to find a way to corrupt that energy so that it simply doesn't make a difference, meaning if you have a strong mission to fulfill, it will be waiting to attack. You might think it is a little unfair that we're born so fragile and almost thrown into an ocean full of sharks, but that's the life we chose when we decided to come here. We chose to come to this school to learn from the challenges that our soul must go through to ascend to a new level of greatness. In case you were not aware, this isn't the only planet that exists, and it's not the best planet to be living on, but we are here for a reason. I have seen planets just like ours, but more advanced, just like I've seen planets where an animal species here has their own planet elsewhere... It's infinite, and there is no impossible. Just because a few are waiting on proof of other existence does not mean those who are connected need scientific proof. When you connect, you can connect with any kind of energy in the universe, just pick your frequency. I like to think that if someone imagined it, it must be real somewhere. I don't believe we "create" ideas; I believe we "download" them. Our energy is this infinite story of information passed along from our past lives and our lineage, like a memory drive without limit.

So, when we are born, our perception is opened, our sensitivity is opened, our third eye is opened, our pureness and our energy life is infinite. The more time we spend on earth as the years go by and we are growing up, not only is our energy being fed by those who care for us at first, but we're also this beautiful little sponge absorbing every bit of information and examples we can because our mind is learning. It is the times when we begin to be censored, deprived, suppressed, when our energy begins to be dimmed or put into vulnerable states. It's the times when we were introduced to something other than our innocence, we were exposed to harm, pain, and sadness. You see, the moment that as a child you go through a vulnerable state, which can happen if you're very roughly yelled at, or you're neglected, or you go through a moment of deep sadness... These are the moments when your perfect circle of protection around you, the one meant to be given by your caretaker's cracks and negative entities, make their way in. This is why it's so important for anyone who chooses to be a parent to make sure that no matter what a child does, they should never be put in a situation of uncontrollable crying or selflessness, to not break the energy protection and make the child vulnerable. Always teach with love and discipline, patience, but also firmness.

I know this because my first possession was at the age of eight after being yelled at and crying feeling helpless or unwanted, at this moment something jumped into my body and pushed me to the floor. From that day on, I became a rebellious little girl. Never make a child feel unwanted, unloved, helpless, or worthless; these will immediately break their protective shield.

We are a flexible and elastic tube from our genitals to our throat, which is the passage of energy and electricity.

Birth

Birth is supposed to be the most pleasurable experience for a woman. Bringing life into this world. Her ultimate gift. The reason we have our genitals is basically to create. Any pain that happens during birth is transferred to the baby as a birth trauma. These emotions of pain pass through to the newborn in its most vulnerable state, when it moves from the spiritual world to the physical world. Considering we have already been absorbing feelings and information before we are even born, it is crucial for pregnancies to be full of love and peace.

Imagine if the first known human emotion we are introduced to is pain and trauma, screaming, aggressive movements, and taps on our backs. This is something that records itself in our subconscious, the first known emotion we learned was pain and suffering, and if we couldn't be delivered naturally, we received help entering this world, which is our first lesson; we need help to do anything in life.

Hospitals are full of women with health problems, many of them originating from sex, and they do not even know it. This is where our research started. How can sex affect our health and birth?

The reality is that if our physical channel (body) is fully opened and with no traumas, it can deliver a perfectly healthy baby in a most pleasurable time. You might have heard of incredibly young women delivering babies in a bathroom without knowing what just happened. When the female body is healthy, it has the perfect ability to stretch and tighten with no trauma or pain. Just like there is control of the throat, there should also be control of the yoni; it's how we are built and what nature decided for us until we went against it.

Pain is what happens when our channel begins to close. When I say channel, I mean from your mouth to the tip of your genitals, for women, the lips, for men, the tip. This unfortunately closes when we have sexual encounters that generate negativity. It is as if you are a fluorescent light stick, and a bug enters; it dims a part of that light. The same thing happens with us in real life. If we begin using our sexual energy early in life, meaning while our puberty is still happening, then we have the risk of being deceived or heartbroken because our capacity to make good decisions is still in process. When a deception happens, this is when negativity is created, and it begins as one blockage. Remember we are light, and darkness is always waiting for a strike. The whole purpose of negativity's existence is closing channels, so people give birth in traumatic conditions and creates cycles of broken generations, closing channels of light so there is more darkness in the world.

You come from listening to everything your parents talked about while you were in the womb. This is your first programming. Did you hear love? Or rejection? Did your parents want you? Did they want a boy instead of a girl? This is your seed in life, and because we can't expect to hold them accountable, we need to later act on healing those wounds that are in our subconscious and affect our everyday life.

Now, having birth trauma doesn't mean you are born with negativity. It only means you have more weak links, so when you are growing, you will be a little more susceptible to negative energy than others. For example, if a baby is born in very painful conditions with difficulties, they will have dents in their energy, but later can manage to live a fulfilling, positive life if they are surrounded by positiveness.

If they are surrounded by negativity, they will be more likely to have these traumas arise from their genes. Bad genes awake when traumatic situations occur, and negativity sparks them. So, in other words, if you come from an alcoholic family and are raised within that environment, you will be more exposed to toxic energy, which will find a way to awaken your negative genes. Negative energy knows your weakness, and if we have traits (illnesses, promiscuity, alcohol, drugs, failure, phobias, traumas), it will work its way to us to awaken those genes. This is why your gene pool isn't responsible for the negative genetics; you or whoever raised you is responsible for awakening the negative genes within you. These only wake up when fed. If you are fed with love and positive energy, only the positive genes will arise; if you have traumatic moments, those moments will trigger a negative gene.

We need to have a perfectly elastic channel, especially in the genitals for women, so that energy, life, can constantly flow through there. Having elasticity at the core is very important for a healthy body and channel. This results in feeling only pleasure and no pain. Nothing but pleasure should ever be felt in the woman's genitalia.

Circumcision is a modification of humans by humans. Nature made man with a foreskin naturally. The removal of the skin was implemented by a religion and then doctors from that religion started recommending it as more hygienic, which is ridiculous because you can keep it clean like any other part of your body. This "trend" became popular only to maintain a male dominance over society. In reality, the tip, which is the most sensitive part of the body, should be covered, because when it's exposed, it scrapes on clothing, making it lose sensitivity, making men more aggressive towards their partners. You might disagree but just know whatever feeling you have could be stronger, you just need to concentrate a little more to regain sensitivity, just like women.

Nature made man perfect. Anything humans do to alter perfection is a manipulation of perfection without necessity.

Birth aid started happening when women lost information about sex. Also, the economic need to create more jobs created specialists in fields that were never needed before and would not be needed if a culture of nature was still alive. We must break the cycle of consumption even in the medical field and get back to our natural state as much as possible.

If you want to heal from your birth onward, the following exercise is very simple but might take time.

Exercise

Find yourself in a quiet space where you are sure there will be no interruptions, dark if possible, or with eye covers. Find a comfortable position where you can get into a deep meditative state. Like any meditation, start by relaxing your body muscle by muscle, until you feel no more tension in the position you choose. When you are comfortable enough, you will command yourself to take you to your birth state. You need to set an intention for the practice before you go deep, so to do so, you will first go to the first image that comes to mind as far as you can consciously remember. Be present in that thought and then try to go farther back.

I know you think you won't remember, but everything we ever go through is implanted in our brains; all we have to do is access it. Our mind will forget anything that doesn't give us dopamine. Our survival instinct will block away moments that happened, but if we remember them, and they will only cause harm, it automatically hides them. So, you can access anything you want, all you need is concentration and willingness. Where there is will, there is progress.

If you can't get to that space in time in your first practice, don't lose hope and keep trying. You will imagine yourself inside your mother's womb, imagine the warmth, the liquid, the safety, even crawl into your child pose if needed. Focus on your memory until it becomes a reality. Try to see if you hear anything or feel anything that you can become aware of. Then say you want to experience your birth moment. You want to relive this moment as much as you can. When you do, if you do, after the feeling, you will imagine yourself being born in a place of peace, quiet, warmth, without assistance, breathing on your own, feeling safe. If you aren't able to access the memory of your birth, you will simply imagine a beautiful birth, repeatedly, until your mind records this as a reality. What you are doing is replacing memories with ones that will benefit you most.

I recommend doing this with someone who can guide you through the process of regression. But, if you want to try it alone, you may do so if you let someone know so they can be attentive to your needs. This delicate practice is one where you should not be disturbed, and if you need assistance, there should be no speaking, only the presence of a hand on your arm will be enough for you to feel safe. These practices should not be taken lightly, as everyone has a different ability to access these moments, some faster than others. It all depends on how open you are spiritually and how vulnerable you allow yourself to be. Being in the presence of a loved one or a spiritual guide, in my opinion, is always recommended for safety, since we don't want you to fall into a moment of despair without anyone to comfort you. So, only you know what you are capable of and how powerful your mind is to achieve these exercises.

Puberty

In your childhood years, you are learning and protected, as long as you don't go through traumatic moments that put you in a vulnerable state, you will be okay. For those that go through vulnerable stages, it will just require tougher endurance in your healing process further on, especially in puberty.

The moment you go through puberty is the moment when your body and the ether decide it's time for you to begin the process of detaching the responsibility of the energy from your parents and slowly begin to thrive from the energy on your own, based on your personal experiences. The process doesn't happen immediately, and you will always be attached energetically to your parents, but when you hit puberty and a few years after, the more those responsibilities will become yours alone and this is when your own personal karma journey begins. Puberty in a spiritual world is the process of your sensitive spots awakening on their own. You feel this spark of energy in your heart area that reflects in your third eye and genitals. You start becoming aware of your sensitive spots in a stronger way and relate them to a more physical response, which you associate with the word arousal.

Now, suddenly, the peace you are supposed to feel all the time, being in the umbrella of your parents, is something you have to start generating on your own by becoming your own power source, where your decision will make you or brake you. Adulthood really happens fully once development and puberty are finished. In between, we go through some of the most defining moments of our lives. Whatever happens when we are in the state of detachment from our parents' energy is something our body will adapt to as its own, like a teaching. For example, if when you are going through puberty you take up alcohol, drugs, sex... while your organs and body are finishing their development cycle, it will take these up as a habit which will be ingrained in your body's system, making it harder to get rid of when you become an adult. If you pick up any of those habits after puberty, your body will have enough strength to protect itself from negative vices.

I always give people the example of penetration at an early stage of our body's development. Imagine you're baking a cake; you have a specific time to leave the cake inside the oven so it's fully cooked, and you do the toothpick test to make sure no crumbs come out when you poke it. It's simply not ready yet and needs a little more time to develop. That's exactly what happens to the female's yoni, what happens to the body's liver with alcohol, and our neurons with drugs. So, you can understand how crucial it is for this migration of energy responsibility and development to be as flawless and perfect as possible. Nature is perfect. In the real world we are in, most teenagers go through rough years in their puberty, making it harder to break patterns later, but not impossible.

The moment our bodies start experiencing the shocks of generating energy on our own is when we feel those butterflies and currents rushing through our bodies like an adrenaline rush. Unfortunately, most people don't have this information, so they think it's an adrenaline rush that they can't handle, and they end up releasing this energy through early intercourse. With the proper teachings and information, this is a perfect time for people to be involved in sports so they can burn some of that energy out physically and activate their sexual energy properly by practicing tantric meditations and practices.

Ideally, we should start practicing sexual energy practices physically at this stage, either alone, with a trusted companion, a toy, or even a peeled cucumber if we want to use nature's way. Don't feel weird, women stick toxic plastic up their bodies, so a cucumber should make sense.

Cucumber juice acts like a perfect hydration for the yoni walls, and you can find different sizes. Cucumbers proven by us are the best natural remedy for the yoni canal, the piece has to press firmly against its walls for about 5 to 10 minutes as often and needed as possible. This can be practiced at any age during or after puberty, depending on the person's development. This is the time when knowledge of sexual energy should be learned. Understanding and learning to create energy, not to have sex, or to mistake the act of elevating and generating energy with the act of sex. Having a conscience of what is happening and embracing the electricity for progress, not to release, nor just focus on the carnal feeling. Pleasure comes in many forms, in ways of life, companionship, affection, and not just sexual. By learning how to move this energy, you will then have no lust when you meet the other gender, because your energy will be in balance and not all concentrated at your lower root or genitals. This will benefit you in not making mistakes and sharing your energy out of lust with just anyone, plus it will maintain your elasticity, keeping your body healthy for a better future and a healthy birth later.

When people start to experience sexual acts at a very early age with the mixture of different companions sexually, they unfortunately lose the sensitivity of some Energy spots or cripple their activation altogether. The body has thousands of sensitive spots to generate energy, but approximately 130 main ones. When any of those thousands of points get caressed, you will feel an incredible amount of pleasure in the whole body, without even the need for penetration. From the top of our head to the end of our feet. The reality is that those sensitive spots need to be fed with positive energy to flourish and channel positive energy. If there is some kind of negative act involved, like, for example, unwanted sexual acts or relationships that are toxic that generate any kind of negativity, those actions create traumas and atrophies in the body and energy. In other words, any act that you do at a stage where your energy is awakening (puberty) that contributes to the generation of negativity will, in fact, weaken your energy spots and loosen your positive energy connection. Now, let's say that you are one of those few people who are blessed enough to find their loved one and soulmate at a very young age. Maybe you do become active sexually early, but since it's with the same stable and loving relationship, with acts filled with love, it won't have any negative effect on your growth. Here, your body's chemistry will get used to one person for the rest of its life, so it's perfect.

The most important part of all of this activity comes from intention, caring, and loving, not being aggressive. It's very rare to have a sexual situation where the man has care or love, or respect for the girl, and treats her with kindness, it's usually the other way around, men treat women with aggression because that is either what they've learned to do in porn videos or simply because they are venting their stress on to the woman, causing or influencing the cycle of a broken female lineage within that family specially in puberty where everything is tender and gentle. A man who loves does not feel the need to be aggressive. This is where the lack of information and learning how to have sex through porn ruined society.

Let's not forget the oppression that women have come from in generations before. Many of our ancestors went through situations of rape. Unfortunately, in case you don't know, we carry the weight of our ancestors in our genes when it's time for us to make decisions. So, for example, if you come from a family line where not just in the line of your direct parents, but even further along your lineage, there was some type of trauma, you already have a major possibility to be inclined negatively somehow within that topic of trauma. If you look closely, it's very normal for family cycles to repeat themselves until one decides to cut the line. All we need to do is become aware of them. Is there something you think you made choices on that wasn't necessarily your own?

The right way to go through puberty would be to keep very active in physical activities so that the moving energy can be discharged. Remember our channel is from mouth to core, so breathing heavy like you do in sports will exhale energy out and release the tension at your pelvic area. Once your body goes through the full development process, then it will stabilize itself, not giving you sudden rushes that you can't handle. Everything is getting used to.

Another very good exercise to practice is breath work and meditation, conscious activities like yoga, as well, help energy flow in the body, and definitely go hand in hand with strength and flexibility. Women need to purchase a toy or find someone of trust to exercise channeling energy with, which also helps to keep the elasticity of the yoni rings and wall. Tantric meditation is highly recommended at this stage, which is basically acknowledging the spark that's working and controlling its flow upwards in the body towards the brain, so this way you can alleviate the pressure off the genital area. It's almost as if your body is releasing sparks of electricity on its own until it finally stabilizes and just has a constant flow. The body needs to adapt, like everything in life.

The more you can maintain this energy flow inside of you, releasing it towards physical activity and mental work, the more connected you will be further on. This is the difference between people who seem to just flow with everything in life and people who are constantly bumping into walls because their connection is having a shortage. It's almost as if an electric cable were having voltage loss, so you have less abundance.

Something else that affects our future physically is the lack of ability our body has to heal itself and create antibodies. According to our doctor who worked with us for over sixteen years, he was able to prove throughout the time with his patients that women and men who had a busy and mixed sexual life in puberty have a weak immune system. This happens because the body is supposed to get used to a different person's chemistry, absorb it, and create antibodies for the other person's genes. This can be related to the smell you give off when you have sex with someone; if your bodies are in sync there should be no smell during or after sex. If our body is in development and we unite it with someone else's fluids, our body will understand that it needs to evaluate and create antibodies for that person's genetic pool. From their saliva to intimate fluids, our bodies take time to create these antibodies, and around three months later, damage their sexual organs and accustom themselves to this style of sex, and not soft lovemaking. Men will have risks of molding their lingam to only channel negativity, losing sensitivity, and women will risk injuring internal spots.

Your body in development will produce large amounts of discharge; this is pure energy you are channeling anytime. This discharge of fluids is produced by the body's arousal, which is what is lost over the years if the body is not used correctly. It's the corruption of a healthy system.

Something else to keep in mind is that each moment of penetration, even if with the same person, creates peaks of energy. This is your energy making a connection with a different frequency, so those are the moments that mark you the most. So, if these actions are aggressive, you will be left with more negative energy than if you just had one slow penetration.

Today, ninety percent of women are searching for a partner, and it's becoming increasingly difficult for them. Several doctors and psychologists began investigating the cause, but it all comes down to an energetic issue that our meditators have perceived:

When a woman goes through development and the first signs of sexuality appear, something called "the charm" emerges in her. This charm is an energetic reaction that sparks desire in a man. Generating desire means "desiring" the young woman, but not due to sexual attraction, nor with any sexual interest, but simply as a person. generated around the age of seventeen, sometimes eighteen, and in some young people, it produces what is called falling in love without thinking about anything sexual—perhaps just having her by their side is enough to complete their happiness, and it happens equally for both.

Having sexual relationships too early with several partners, when those sensitive points become atrophied, prevents the energy we call "the charm" from being generated, and there is no desire from anyone, only sexual or companionable approaches. Now, this is lifelong, and further down the line, when she has the urge to have sex with someone, she must go out and search for someone, and it becomes very difficult to find them. She finds them, but those who approach her do so for sex, never out of desire. Desire is provoked by that energy called "the charm," which was never allowed to be born in a lot of girls in their youth.

The proven reality so far is that no woman who does not have "the charm" manages to find a man who truly falls in love with her; instead, he will be there for companionship and sexual relief, because the desire for her will be missing. Desire in a male is the concern for her progress and her health, above everything else. In the end everything is possible to recover with the energy of love.

The perfect example which I hope is for future generations, to be able to reach our point of development as purely as possible without the influence of any negative energy in our lives, this way providing a more stable and successful future.

The Tree of Life

Let's look at our life as a tree. Our roots are literally when we grow up; that's the foundation of how solid our trunk is, our basis. From there go our branches, which usually split from the trunk into at least two sides. Let's see one side of the tree as if it were the positive side, the other side as if it were the negative side. Life is divided into positive and negative; you get to choose which one you want to exist in.

The positive side will be filled with happiness, health, and love but it will be hard work to achieve those things. The negative side will be filled with richness, short dopamine moments, and lust. Now you can also make mistakes, swerve to a negative side, and after a while, you realize, and you get back on track. The bad thing is when you've been on the negative side for a very long time. It takes you longer to get back up, but it's not impossible. Every decision we make constantly changes the outcome of our current story, so we are constantly writing our story. It's important to find balance in things.

Our roots are the most important part of our lives and what will decide how long we will live and how prosperous we will be. If our foundation is weak, we will need constant care and possibly need ongoing help.

When you have an excess of something, your body won't get as much pleasure from it. If you like chocolate, eating it every day will most likely make you need a break from it. Eat when your body needs food, when it makes you feel hungry. If we overfeed ourselves, our mind no longer associates with the pleasure of feeding and just gets used to constant food and a nonstop digestive system. Why give our body food if it's working on something else and hasn't requested it? Sleep when you feel like sleeping, have sex when you feel like generating energy, not for the mere carnal feeling, but to connect with a higher realm, to prosper.

Mental Programming

Just like our body is going through its developmental stage, the mind is also growing with it; the difference in the mind is that it's constantly learning. If you know anything about electricity imagine a 220-circuit breaker on your head and another one on your genitals, they are the ones that feed the electricity in your body, meaning energy. So, you start with a large voltage, you want to be able to maintain it, not lower it. The mind is something that is always connected, its own galaxy, which you can travel through and discover new conscious connections.

To expand our consciousness, we need to be at that stage of pure connectivity. So, reprogramming our minds, no matter our age, is necessary. Of course, the older you are, the longer it will take to wipe out the hard drive and rewrite it, but it's not impossible. Some live for years by intense ideologies and customs, so if you are in that group, it will take a little more time, because you get to be so utterly convinced of what you have been taught that it becomes a way of life. If you are younger, it will be very easy for you to pick and choose what you want to adopt into your way of life. After you become an adult, you should question everything. Now you understand that you have a choice of following your parents' ideologies or not. A family that wants your personal growth will never condition you to their love; they will allow you to be free and become your own person with your own choices. Family, just as people should be viewed always in perspective, meaning just because they're your family does not make them right on everything, and does not make them your owner. Some people fear thinking outside of the box because of the backlash they might get for not following family traditions like certain religions and beliefs. But just ask yourself these questions... Would someone who unconditionally loves you and is correctly connected to positive energy only ever suppress something that makes you happy? Or force something that makes you unhappy? This is creating the same mistakes generation after generation. You are your own master of your energy and should decide what is best for your soul's spiritual growth. Don't feel pressured by ancestral weights, as they lived in a different time than you. The energy of the planets was totally different and aligned differently. So, feel free to reprogram your mind. This basically means, question everything you have ever been taught for as far as you can remember. This will take some time, but it's worth it.

    The best way to know which of these customs strains us from spiritually growing is very simple. Which one of the most common ideologies in your life makes you unhappy? Start from there. There is always enough, but in reality, you don't even need to meditate if your channel is high in vibration because every thought you consciously have already has a reaction in the universe. So, for those trying out the law of attraction, which by the way, was one of the books that changed my life, if you are trying out the visions of what you want, but your body's channel is half blocked or empty, no matter how many hours a day you think of something it will be very far away from you to reach. Whereas, if you worked on your sexual energy as a priority then you would see a much faster result. The mind is the one that guides the energy that your body generates. Remember that.

EXERCISE

Make a list on the following page of the things you would like to change. The sayings that you constantly repeat that are attracting failure to your life, the "don'ts, can'ts, or not enough".

For every one phrase, you will replace it with:

You can't	I can
There is not enough	There is abundance
There is no money	Thank you for my abundance
You're not good enough	I am the best at what I do because I do it with love
I'm not worth it	I love myself so others can love me
No one loves me	I am never alone
I'm stupid	I am wise
I'm ugly	I am beautiful

Even if you laugh at what you are saying, just by saying it, you are already feeding your mind this reality, until one day it will become a reality, but it must start with your affirmations. Just twist the words around.

YOUR TEXT

The exercise you will do to reprogramming your mind from things you would like to be free from, one by one, is the following:

Always start with a conscious view of something that connects you to positivity first. An image, a person, a place, focus.

Take a deep breath through your nose, hold it for 4-7 seconds, and blow it out, pushing like you are deflating. Repeat as many times as needed to bring enough oxygen to your brain so you can then focus on your overall state. Bring awareness to your body, and notice if there is any tension you need to release. Tension can distract you, so be in a comfortable position.

Close your eyes, thinking of this: What is something that is part of my life that I would like to leave behind that makes me unhappy? Then be aware of how thinking about it makes you feel. Be aware of how your stomach or abdominal area feels, if there is any tension or density. Every emotion we hold is an energy space inside of us. Now that you've located the physical reaction of this emotion, I want you to take a deep breath again, gently, and repeat to yourself:

"I appreciate the effort of those teaching me, but I have decided it's now my time to choose what is right for me through my own experiences."

With every deep breath you take, and after this affirmation, you will start to blow out this tension in your body that belongs to this one subject or saying. Every time you push out, it's getting further away from you, your body is relaxing, and you feel great, full of open space to learn new things. You will have to do this several times and for each phrase you want to change. But in between, you will wake up to the following affirmations:

"Thank you for another day, for life, thank you for so much abundance, thank you for so much abundance, thank you for so much abundance". "Today I will be aware of my feelings when I am doing something that doesn't feel good with me and when this happens, I will take a deep breath, be grateful for the awareness and change my pattern of thought to that which makes me happy and fulfilled". I am in control.

The idea is for you to remove data in your brain that is not causing you a reaction of progress. Just like when you wipe out your phone or computer from cache or unwanted data, it's exactly what you want to be doing with your brain. Don't save any unwanted information and leave room for new information that can enrich you.

With so much processing going on in your brain throughout the day, it's difficult to reprogram your mind fast enough to make a lot of changes. You would need to move out of loud places and allow your mind to be quiet and peaceful more often. But you will go as fast as you can and as steady as possible. Meaning, no brakes. It can take weeks, months, or years. It all depends on how deeply rooted your beliefs are and your perseverance.

Your body and mind are mainly in an automatic mode throughout the day, where a large percentage of the things you do in your day you do without even being fully aware of them. It's as if you were in auto mode. You drive to your job and don't even realize what you just passed. Imagine this being your life in general, where life passes you by, and you haven't noticed a glimpse of it. If you can't make out a single difference from your trip to work yesterday to the one today, then you are in auto pilot and this is not living in the present, this is you lost in connection. By alarming or commanding your mind when you wake up to make you aware of these moments, you are leaving an order in your subconscious to trigger every time something that's off happens, so you can start to be more aware of your thoughts and feelings throughout the day, and in the end be more present and aware.

You can do this with personality traits, like anger, frustration, guilt, fear, anxiety, and depression. Most of the time, you go through those because you have no control over your energy stabilization in your body. Having an open channel also means full control of the energy flow within your body, control of your emotions, which very few people have.

As you progress in time with each little trait to change or reprogram, you will continue to the next. Where you can be more specific like: "I want to be aware if I become angry, I'm sending energy towards becoming more peaceful every time". There will come a time when this happens more often than you think, and by discovering the time of day in which it happens, you're already training your subconscious to alert you when something negative happens within you. The trick is to use both our subconscious and our conscious together. Most of the time, the brain is making purely subconscious decisions motivated and ruled by ideas we have ingrained in our minds. This is why it's so important to filter out what we learn and choose to keep. You should start seeing the difference in the first week or so if you are doing it right.

It's basically commands of recording to your subconscious. Our subconscious is most highly active when we are asleep; it's why we can dream, which is really connecting to other parallel realities.

So, you want to try to get to the point where you can have a perfect balance of both.

When you dream very lucid and awake dreams you are in a more balanced state of mind between subconscious and conscious. Your dreaming state is where your loved ones or energies from other dimensions know they can communicate with you. Sometimes you might even see visions of the past or future.

If you try to program your mind every time you wake up and every time you go to sleep, commanding functions, you are slowly teaching your conscious self to control the subconscious, which is the one that works for you most of the time. When we allow ourselves to make choices based on intuition, we are allowing the universe to speak through us and make wiser choices. Not choices based on common sense taught by society, but by intuition.

Exercise

In programming your mind to release past traumas, you will do the following exercise:

Find a comfortable, quiet place where there are no distractions. Take a deep breath on 3 counts through your nose, hold it for 3 seconds, and blow it out, pushing for 3 or more seconds. Repeat as many times as needed to bring enough oxygen to your brain so you can then focus on your overall state. Bring awareness to your body. Now repeat internally, "show me what I need to heal", notice the first person or situation that comes to mind. This might take some time, but when you repeat it enough times, the right person or situation should come to mind. The whole purpose of this is to bring your mind to such a state of peace before you start this exercise that when you ask yourself something very specific, you can easily access it because it's already a part of you; you're just always so busy that you don't pay attention to your own feelings or thoughts. I think that one of the most important parts of our day is having self-aware, conscious time with ourselves, to get to know ourselves. To evaluate where we are at this stage and every stage of our lives. If we never take the time to observe how we've grown or how we haven't grown, we can never progress. I think the time when I've grown the most in my life is when I've had time by myself, because you're able to have silence around you throughout the day, so it really allows you to be more self-aware of your reactions, especially if they are reactions that go against the silence and the peace that's around. Just remember that all you have to do is rearrange or change those thoughts. Also, rearrange your interaction with those people whose thoughts don't help you progress. Because at the end of the day, there isn't going to be anyone to blame but yourself. Instead of trying to find who to blame, change that thought to try to find how to make it better. It's time to take on some responsibility and try to find solutions.

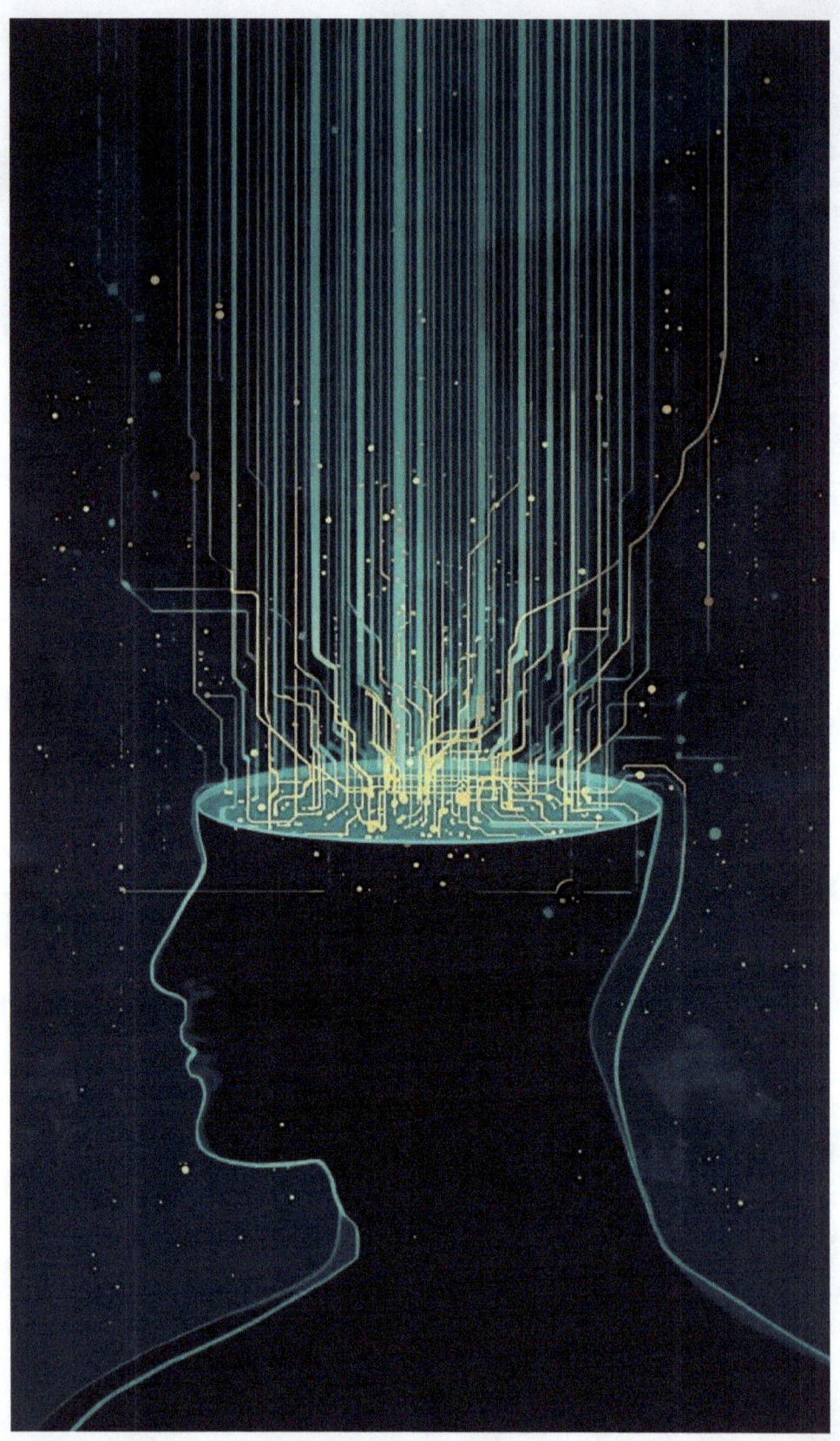

Guided by the Universe

We always plan what we want, how we want it, but only the universe knows how our energy resonates and what our next teaching will be. If we stopped making so many plans, aside from our normal responsibilities, stopped planning ahead, and allowed ourselves to be spontaneous, we could expose ourselves more to situations that we need to live in, in order to progress.

When you're in the same place for a long period of time, your energy will be comfortable. But when you expose yourself to a park, an open space, the ocean, or natural locations, you are entering a space of unknown energy to your vibration. You charge from the place's energy. Which is why, when you travel, I would recommend not traveling to large cities, where you might be entertained, but your energy will not recharge from positivity. Just from all the radiation from electronics and signals you are basically frying yourself.

Natural locations, especially those with water involved, will always benefit the soul more. By exposing your energy to new energy, you will return to your everyday life more relaxed. Schedules are necessary, but when they are done, intuition needs to take over.

Next time you think of traveling, open a map somewhere online or on paper and drop a pin. Allow energy to take you where you need to be. If you can, instead of planning the full trip, just plan the location, then let yourself be relieved from the burden of having to match a plan or an agenda. Just be present in a new space, allow yourself to meet new people, and let the energy guide you, be adventurous, and listen to the cues.

Everyone is so busy planning that they stop living in the moment. You can't possibly think your loved ones, or guardian angels, or whoever is trying to communicate with you, can reach you if you don't give yourself time to just listen, pause, breathe. Disconnect from technology. Disconnect with the world and connect to a new world of wonder where the thrill of being spontaneous leads you right to where you need to be when you need to be there. Stop planning everything.

The last trips I've made were without planning, and whatever I was looking for was just presented to me as I went along at the right time and the right place.

I have too many stories to tell about this particular subject. But I will share one, which I believe was one of the first big opportunities we had. Back in 2014, when we were looking to buy our first house and move out of a shared apartment, we saw a community we loved and said, "That's where we want our house". It's in a very small community, so it was very rare for any houses to go up for sale, and if so, they would disappear in no time. So, I posted a notification alert on the website for home sales just within that community and waited... about 4 months.

We had been following some live auction sales, which we even bid on way higher than we could manage and never won. We were giving up hope in that location because it was simply out of our reach financially. But we continued to focus and say that is where we will live.

Then one night, around 4 am, coming from a late-night job, I see someone uploaded a house for sale in that community right then and there. So, we didn't sleep. At 8 am, we called the number, and it was a Sunday; banks don't work on Sundays. But the realtor agreed to do his first viewing. He said he already had 4 pending offers for the full price, but he had told them to wait until Monday to formally present the offers to the bank. The house was in foreclosure. We went to the location; it was incredibly abandoned and not something, you would jump to say what an amazing place! But we saw through the ugly and made a much lower offer than what was being asked, knowing there were already full price offers on the property. The energy was so much in our favor that it motivated our realtor to call the bank on a

Sunday and talk about how deteriorated the property was and that it would be hard to sell. The bank, being somewhere else and not in the same state, trusted the realtor. Our offer had been dropped about 60k, which the realtor was hesitant about, but he said, "What's the worst that can happen? They will counteroffer". The bank manager not only picked up the phone but also agreed with a counteroffer of 10k more, which was the exact amount of how much we had in our bank account, not a dollar more or less.

We closed a sale on a Sunday, and next Monday we made the transaction. The realtor got the 4 pending offers at full price, and he had to give notice that it was already sold. This brought us a bit of friction in the community because one of the offers was from the association manager who remodeled and resold houses, and this house was said to be the nicest one in the neighborhood and the best location, with no neighbors and next to the guards. On top of that it was sold way undervalued.

Things take time. When we are so anxious and desperate about completing a task or getting what we want, we forget that if it doesn't happen it's because it simply wasn't meant for us. When things are meant for you and you give yourself intuition and generate the proper energy to attract what you want, the right situation will present itself, and everything will fall into place. You just must trust and not doubt. If it takes longer than expected, it's simply because it's not your time. Stop trying to control everything.

You can control your mind to always be grateful for whatever outcome comes your way. Sometimes you just must leave it up to the universe by feeding the thought and desire with positive energy you create. Be awake and aware of the signs around you.

Emotions

You don't have control of your life until you have control of your emotions. Most people are so used to being the way they are that they don't make much of it and continue through life with these traits, which only enable them to attract more negativity. But what most people have is a huge pile of emotional accumulation ready to burst at any time, and usually towards the wrong people, the ones we love.

If you have any recollection of how you used to be when you were younger, take that into consideration for how you should be, without the stress of life and responsibilities. Ironic because we work to become what we are as adults, just to work to get back to how we were as kids.

For the most part, people don't have control of their emotions because they are too busy with entertaining their brains with other things. We don't give time for our brains to think on their own without some kind of external influence. If you go about your day not taking into consideration how you are feeling and just acting out of impulse, then you have zero control of your energy. The truth is that in today's world, most people are also depending on short dopamine shots, and we can thank social media shorts for this. Our body is used to going from laughter to sad to shock in very short time, creating an emotional instability and allowing technology to always control our emotions.

Having control of your emotions is a step closer to having control of your body's energy. If anyone can just come to you and take you away from your state of mind, then you are giving that person control. If you are always out of a peaceful state of mind, then you have lost control of your inner self to negativity. If you or anyone you know acts very impulsively, this is due to negative energies around or within you that are triggering your emotions.

Our emotions mainly bottled up from our stomach upwards. Any non-spoken words and repression you have will bottle up unwanted emotions that will build up something worse in the long run. You don't have to say what's on your mind all of the time, but if something is uncomfortable to you, you should have the discretion of speaking your mind respectfully or speaking it later on to someone else. The point is to get it out. These emotional blockages are the ones you can easily get rid of with breathwork, consciousness, meditation, or voice activation practices.

When we are young, we have no filter, no shame, no fear. Learn to be young again, prioritize your well-being. If you are not well, how can you give a hand to others who depend on you? Having life responsibilities isn't an excuse for not having control of yourself.

The first step to take control of your emotions is to become aware of them. Once you have a moment of anger or frustration, it's already happened; you can't go back. So, take your time before bed for a few minutes and go over your day. Go over the good and the bad, analyze where you can do and be better. Don't spend too much time overthinking a situation, but enough to review it and draw conclusions on where you could have reacted differently.

Give yourself a rule: you cannot be mad or angry or frustrated for more than 3 minutes, then 2, then 1. Depending on how often this happens, you will give yourself leverage on time and move forward from there. Think of a trigger you can create to remind you of being aware of your emotions, like the famous rubber band snap. Wear a rubber band, and when you get off track and react negatively towards something, snap it. There are very practical triggers you can use to make you react to bad emotions; once your mind gets the idea, you will no longer need them. If you spend more than that time feeling these emotions of low vibration, you will only attract more negative situations to your life that you don't need, so make it a game. Sometimes you can't just turn off this attitude, especially if it's been with you for years, but if you have the will, it will adjust slowly towards your stability. You are intelligent, you are wise, so why would you spend time out of your precious life on something that doesn't feel good? You have better things to do and better emotions to feel that enrich you and fulfill you. That is what you are aiming for.

Learning to be selfish with ourselves is not bad. You need to be selfish of your time, your energy, and of your value as a human being. When you value yourself enough, you will only allow situations and people around you to enrich you. If you don't, it simply means you still don't think you deserve the best, and you are not ready to receive it. So, learn to be selfish and put yourself first.

Some of us have this genetic pool of loudness, or attitude, that comes in our blood. I know because I come from a strong attitude lineage, and it took me years to get rid of my nasty attitude, or better yet only use it when needed. But once I started listening to how my body reacted when I was acting out, I was able to control it before it ever happened, until it just didn't fit in with the everyday person I decided to be. It takes time, but remember, whatever it is, you are in control. Nothing should have power over what you want for yourself. Impulses aren't you; they are manipulations.

How much time have you spent trying to have someone accept or believe your point of view over theirs, or trying to prove yourself right to others? Is it necessary for others to think like you do? How much time have you spent worrying about something that is out of your control? Time wasted is energy wasted with only a negative return.

You don't fix things with overthinking. You only become stagnant. Spinning in a circle of confusing energy and moving emotions of worry within you, emotions that move low-vibrating energy that affect your well-being and overall health. So, what if someone is doing something that doesn't fall into your adequate etiquette or norms? Who made us the ultimate preacher?

Most worry so much about other people's problems that they forget to focus on their own path. The system is designed for it to be this way, it's why entertainment and gossip exist, to keep us distracted and focused on others, not on our self-progress. If we don't give ourselves the appropriate balance with things, we simply lose balance. When we are watching a movie or anything on a screen, we are yielding the power of our emotions to that production. They have total control of what you feel for that full 2 hours of time, or however long.

If you bury yourself in entertainment that is based on adrenaline and fear, you will attract energies that are comfortable with those vibrations. Remember that fear makes you vulnerable, so keep in mind that you are watching something fake. If you love watching love movies, you immerse yourself in a vulnerable state and sometimes even lose touch with reality, believing or hoping to have and live what is being shown to you in the movie. I'm not saying not to watch movies, just be aware afterwards that it's a fantasy and not real life. It happens to a lot of stable relationships, the movie ends, and the person starts wondering about what if.

How many times have you watched a horror film and had trouble sleeping? Or how many times have you watched a love story, and when it's over, you wish that was your story? This will make you reject the relationship you are in for a moment, affecting your energy until that effect goes away. See, everything we expose our minds to has the potential to influence the decisions we make in our everyday lives. So, as silly as it might be, reminding ourselves that what we see is just a distraction for some time is all it takes to not let it influence our energy or what we attract. In other words, be smart. If you see a movie about drunk teenage kids and you remember how you were, if that was the case, then you are fueling back the energy you generated at that time. Good or bad. Images that trigger memories trigger back the energy created with those past actions.

A way of knowing if your emotions are out of hand is paying attention to your stomach and gut area, as well as your heart. When you are about to be angry, during and after, you will notice your heart races, your adrenaline rushes, your breath rushes, and you can't think well. This is your body disbalanced, your molecules moving radically instead of in waves and motion. One is a heavy metal wave inside of you, and the other is a classical music type of wave, which one would you say is the healing one?

Learn to listen to your body. When something is happening around you that is moving your molecules the wrong way, meaning your heart is starting to race, your stomach is tightening up, before it goes any higher, take a deep breath and walk away. Come back when your body is relaxed and you are ready to face it in a peaceful manner. Because nothing good comes from forceful situations or altercations, so why waste time? It's the only valuable thing we must take care of...TIME.

Discovering our emotional imbalances has to do with a lot of deep thinking into why. When you are bothered by someone or something that is being told to you and you react towards it, it isn't the person's fault that you feel this way; it's yours. What is it about your self-confidence or weakness that you know you have and need to heal? Most of the time, when we get offended by something, it's because it's hitting a weak spot. Allow yourself to observe your reaction next time you are offended and analyze why you get offended. You should be able to deal with any kind of comment, joke, attack, bullying, sarcasm, and not change your state of mind because you have high self-confidence.

When we are weak or doubting ourselves is when we lose our grounding and stability. The universe will constantly expose you to situations that should make you realize the change that needs to happen within you, so you have a better life. It will expose you to hurtful situations so you can analyze your reactions and become better every day. When someone is trying to offend you, they will only be successful if you believe what they are saying. If you are sure of yourself and what you do and who you are, that confidence will never put you in a vulnerable situation like that. Always dig deeper.

Self-Love

How you see yourself is how others see you. It starts within, because we radiate from inside out. If our energy is unstable or toxic, that is exactly what people will perceive of us. You can be a good person, but being good doesn't mean you are pure and not toxic.

This all goes back to our youth, so mental training is needed. But I can suggest some exercises that you can do to help you feel more confident and comfortable with yourself.

1. Walk around your room or house naked as much as you can.
2. Look at yourself in the mirror naked as often as possible in a natural way.
3. Find a hobby you are good at and enjoy, so you can be surrounded by like-minded people and feel accomplished.
4. Only look at motivational online content, so the algorithm only feeds you this; this way there is no temptation.
5. Practice going to a nude beach or community.

You need to get used to looking at your perfections and imperfections, just like everything in life. When we get used to it, it becomes normal. The more you hide from yourself, the more uncomfortable you will be when exposing yourself to others. You are perfect just the way you are, and what will make you even more perfect is working on vibrating higher and fixing the personality traits you know you must change.

If your self-esteem is low, think back at a time when it was different, or if it was always like this, you must identify why you gathered this persona. This usually goes back to when you were young and didn't get moral support from your loved ones. As kids, we need to feel we are good at doing something and get recognition for accomplishing things. If that wasn't the case, then going back in time to moments when that self-esteem was shattered is unfortunately necessary. You need to relive these moments with an adult mentality and open perspective so you can acknowledge where the root is and decide to reprogram and start fresh.

If you hate your love handles, love that if you ever get sick you have a weight reserve that will help you recover faster. If you are a man and you hate your belly, think of what a great pillow it makes. Everything has a bright side, just start looking for it, even if it doesn't make sense or its ridiculous. It's all about what you make of it, not others.

Self-love is something people usually expect to earn outside, from others. The more popular you are or the more you get used to doing things for the sake of pleasing others, the more you will lose yourself along the way. Why would someone you don't even know have such powerful control over you? You don't need others to prove that you are worthy; you are worthy, no matter what anyone else says. Because people will judge you based on their own level of wisdom. A person who's fulfilled and happy will always value their time and not even worry about others. That's the type of person you want as a friend, and for that, you need to be that.

Surround yourself with people who want to move forward, who aspire to do better, and be better. Why would anyone choose to be around people who enable sedentary lives with no progress? No aspirations, no future, no thrill of living. Every aspect of your time that you give to situations that enrich you is another step towards self-love. Because when happiness, hard work, and progress are what you are used to being surrounded by, then your energy is filled with positive energy, which is love. When you are filled with enough love, you will also accept yourself differently.

Don't ever let anyone talk down to you. You need to inspire respect, even if it makes you look tough on the outside. If you allow people to walk all over you, you will never reach self-love. You have every right to stand up for yourself. You are valuable and important, and if you have never heard it before, read this sentence several times until you believe it. It starts in your gut. When you feel it within, it means you are creating energy towards that feeling, making it a reality.

By having confidence in ourselves, we send out a more powerful energy when we think of things we need; it's an energy of power, not a weak vibe of insecurity and shame.

Gratitude	**Affirmations**
Thank you for who I am	☐ I am capable of achieving my goals and dreams.
Thank you for what I have	☐ I radiate confidence, strength, and positivity.
Thank you for who I have	☐ Every challenge I face is an opportunity for growth.
Thank you for my health	I am worthy of love, success, and happiness.

Thank you for so much abundance.

Thank you for today. I choose joy, peace, and progress in all I do.

Beauty

You get used to feeling the way you feel. The older you get, the stiffer your body becomes, doing less, moving less, censoring yourself because you believe you become less because society has told you so when in reality you become more. You become wiser, brighter, and fuller. The flesh is left behind, but the wisdom follows through to infinity. We have been taught that beauty is what we see in every commercial, magazine ad, and movie as an example to follow.

Why is there so much research into illnesses, but very little or none teaching us how to use our energy to heal ourselves? The negativity hovering around us incites us to glorify something physical and allows hollowness to become normal and popular amongst us. When was the last time you heard a popular song today with an actual positive message?

Beauty today is flipped completely from what it really is, which is inner shine. The positivity that radiates from your body should be your beauty. So, we are deceived by darkness to follow looks when the reality is that beauty is how much energy you radiate from within.

The moment you start to feel insecure, heavy, or tense, just relax and remember energy flows through your body so much more when you relax. Life is better when you learn to flow without so much tension. Your life's focus should be on how you can be and do better as a person. In the journey of fulfilling yourself, you will be adding beauty to your soul from the courage of becoming stronger and better every day.

Embrace pleasure as a part of a constant feeling, so your body is connected, and you feel a perfect flow of energy traveling through your body. Open up and let go...

When you get used to seeing everything through the eyes of someone beautiful then everything you see becomes beautiful because life is beautiful. Now if you are constantly going through a vision of shallowness and carelessness, that is exactly what you will be vibrating with, so you will be exposed to it more often.

When beauty reflects from your thoughts to your acts, you will eventually be surrounded by beauty. Where everything you do is with love, every you see as a challenge has a solution, and having that security in yourself that everything will always be all right.

Don't be blinded by beauty; by the time you allow your perception to take over, it might be too late.

Negativity

Negativity is something that's a part of this world because people are constantly aiding to generate more of it. So, everyone complains about how the world is going yet, they do very little to better themselves as beings. Every negative action creates a reaction; every positive action creates a reaction as well. It's common sense. Negative energy being the one mostly created because it's created by sex without love or consciousness.

To be guarded from negativity, we must always have our positive energy at its highest. The moment you lose strength and become vulnerable is when these energies hover around you.

When you are around someone, the strongest way of receiving negativity is through a full body transfer, meaning sexually. But you can also absorb negative energy through toxic work environments, toxic relationships, nightclubs, or places where substances are a priority. You also absorb negative energy simply by being near someone negative, through their eyes, touch, or even more strongly through a kiss. Kissing is underrated. The truth about kissing is that it's as strong a transfer as if you were having penetration. These are the ends of the channel.

Negativity is mostly active when people are under the influence of some substance. This is because substances put the host in a vulnerable state, and negativity doesn't ask permission. When you are under the influence, with that feeling you were searching for of letting go and feeling free, it makes you vulnerable to energies around you and a key target to be attacked. In fact, it will purposely possess one person so it can be transferred to another, like a parasite. If you ever find yourself in a situation with someone who is intoxicated, and acting very wild and sexually, these are the moments when you should back away. These moments are usually completely controlled by negativity and are the ones you will absorb the most. In fact, those who drug and rape others end up repossessing themselves with more negativity. It's the ripple of the actions that attracts the reactions.

The most vulnerable stage you can be in is the stage of arousal, or substance influence, this is when you finally allow your conscious mind to take a break and let yourself be guided by the feeling of pleasure in your body. This is the highest state of meditation there is. So, if you are generating negative energy, imagine how easy it is for this energy to filter through to your body. You can't feel pleasure if you are uptight. So, when this happens, you need to be in a safe space with people who feel safe.

When you become vulnerable enough to feel as much pleasure as possible, that's when you want to make sure that what's around, you is positive. This way, your result will be progress and not being stuck.

What generates negativity, you might ask?

Anything that doesn't originate from pure thought. Meaning anything influenced by negative energy is no longer your own pure thought. See, we are positive beings; we just get contaminated by traveling through life in a world that's corrupt. Your thought of origin would always be to care for and respect one another. Negativity made sure that in some households this wasn't present and taught some people to be aggressive, abusive, deceiving, or lying to people just so it can spread.

If your action comes from love and a good intention, it will always generate positivity. If your feelings are being distorted and you are getting feelings of anger, aggression, hate, or anxiety, they will make you act accordingly.

The same situation applies to the place you are living in. If you just moved into a house and months later you start getting sick, can't sleep, or your personality has changed. This is a demonstration of what you are absorbing in that house or with that new partner you might have. It's important to do reviews of our self-progress every so often to evaluate where you are and analyze how any new people or situations might have changed your energy for the better or worse. Most of the time when we are looking for help or seeking answers, we start the question with the answer. So, if you are asking yourself, 'Is "x" good for me?', you already have the answer. When things are right, you wouldn't doubt it. Your questioning proves the insecurity you have about the situation. You shouldn't take part in anything that causes you to be insecure. Move on, maybe it's time for you to focus on yourself more, because you have all the answers; all you need to do is listen to yourself more.

      People will always give recommendations coming from their own personal perspective, which leads to the conclusion they took to give you that advice. Our opinions are based on personal experiences because you don't know anything aside from your own experiences. Today, you decide on something solely based on information you have read or seen online, but very rarely lived. Your opinion on something today might just be totally different a few years from now; that's meant to happen. We all have a pace at which we move in, according to our surroundings, so don't expect to understand things that are not yet at your level or understand those that don't get what level you are at.

Energetical Vampires could be any of us, really. These are people that have drained their energy so much they have lost all connection to the ether, so they depend on feeding on other people's energies to exist or feel better. How do you feel when you meet a certain person? Do they make you feel good? Are you happy to be around them? How do you feel afterwards? Do things happen after you see them? Good or bad? Do you have a headache? These are all questions that you should be asking yourself to identify any energetic vampires around you. They don't do this because they mean to; it's totally involuntary. If you have enough energy to give off, then it won't affect you, but if you are going through difficult situations, you want to save as much energy as you can. Being surrounded by people who need your energy is not what you want, unless you are a light worker and want to help others. For the most part, all you have to do is limit your time with them. Sometimes, there are people like this in your family that you simply can't totally cut ties with, so you will meet them with grace and patience and recover later. Everyone else, cut ties.

Negativity goes hand in hand with things that come easily. If you want fast money, you may become involved with opportunities that aren't necessarily in positive environments, and since it's just for the money, you won't be fulfilling your accomplishment void. Lies, deceits, scams, cheats, aggression, hate, jealousy, anger, hysteria, are all part of a negative lifestyle. Negative energy feeds off of each and every person when these emotions happen. We have allowed this to happen for quite some time now. Find what fulfills you in every way. Deep inside, your intuition always tells you when something isn't right.

Negativity will also try to sneak itself in through the people you most trust and love. Remember, we are all unique and vulnerable in our own ways. It can happen that if you have someone close who is easily manipulated, it will make sure to use its ways to send a message to you through them so that you take the wrong path. Always be vigilant. When you make decisions, don't ever do them because they are being told to you; do them because you are convinced of them, and they feel good within.

The easiest way for negativity to influence people today is by making them feel like they are in love. If you ever feel like you are in love in a very intense lust situation, the first few times you meet someone, this will usually last only a few months. It's how long negativity needs to affect your life; once it's done so, the lust will fade out, and you are back to the same pattern. You need to take your time when you meet someone; sharing your energy with another should be sacred and done only with love. By giving yourself some time, you will allow yourself to know the person a little better and study if your feelings are, in fact, guided by something positive. Negative energy situations and encounters will always be the wild one, the crazy, the adrenaline rush. It will feel good momentarily but have bad consequences.

If you have negative energy in your body, it will start to slowly block out any positive inclinations you might have towards an abundant life. So instead of wanting something good, you will want and be attracted to something that is not beneficial for your life. Negative resonates with negative.

Traumas are a magnet for negative energy. It's why it's so important to treat them and beat them. The best way to beat negativity is with your intelligence. Negative energy is more known for acting on impulses rather than rational decisions.

So, a thought of aggression of any kind flashing into your mind when you are in the middle of something totally opposite to that thought, should bring a clear response that this thought does not belong to you. Our mind is moved by energy, so any energies around us that want to influence us will send waves to our mind to have "ideas". Just like any loved one can also communicate with us, we just aren't always aware.

In negative energy, this is when, in extreme cases, you have people acting on some of those horrible ideas and end up taking lives; they always say the demons made them do it. If you are weak-minded and broken, you are an easy target for energy manipulation. It happens to most people daily, more often to those who are surrounded by dark energy and in locations where negativity reigns. We just need to learn to identify when a negative emotion happens so we can examine the origin and dismiss it as an external influence. Just aim to have control of your mind, body, and decisions. Aim to be more open, literally, open your mind to receive only good messages.

I believe negativity has done an intense job of infiltrating its way into our lives. We have allowed it to with music, shows, and entertainment. Specifically, the lack of sexual energy education and the totally opposite being promoted: Sexual liberty, which is, in the end, the end of positive energy.

The fastest and easiest way for negative forces to enter your space today is through lust and sex. When negative energy is generated, the process is the same sexually; molecules move, often endorphins move more quickly. There's more pleasure, a greater desire to continue without letting the body rest. Negativity causes much more pleasure or desire to persist than positivity, as positivity works only for the exact amount of time the body and energy need. This defines sex and love.

Sex is our weakness because it knows that if it can make you feel stronger surges of energy for a limited period (meaning strong arousals), that's all it needs for you to be confused and allow it in because you confuse lust with love.

Just be a little more vigilant and less shallow.

Radical impulses of negative emotions are clear proof of negativity inside your body and around you.

When there are days of negative energies coming into our solar system, these usually make you feel dim, sad, and without strength. A few days after these negative energies entering you will always see attacks, aggression in people, rape, and lots of negative sex. This is what we need to balance.

Every thought you have of kindness, love, affection, honesty, and peace generates positive energy. Now, imagine if you are just thinking of it, how much higher it would be if you were using all your body to create it. From your mouth with voice, to your body with motion and feeling, and your mind with thought. Combine all these together, and it's the perfect state of energy generation, usually known as sex.

If you want to create positive energy in your life, you must be aware that it's created in stages and frequencies. Meaning that if you only create positive energy in one act in your life, you still have many other acts to cover. So, it's about becoming a better version of yourself so that you can generate more positive energy along the way effortlessly.

A lot of people blame life for the things that happen to them, but everything is self-created. The only things you had no control over were when you were under the wing of your parents or caretakers. After that, it's all on you. You need to create positive energy for positive things to happen to you. If this energy is not created, then there is nothing to fuel that "request," or "wish," or "prayer" because there is no prime matter, which is the positive energy. You manifest positive energy to the universe; it becomes like a deposit box for your energy, and that is what you will use to make your petitions come alive. It's all YOU. You are your energy source. The ideal of belief in religions was created so people would feel dependent on something else and lose faith in themselves. Psychologically, it's believed that everyone needs to believe in something. But the truth is, all you need to believe in is yourself. That is what makes things happen. Fill your bucket with positive energy so things happen to you. Take it like a game: how much positive energy did I create today? Make it a daily goal, the same as if you were saving money in a bank. Except this is much more important because it will bring so much more than just money in the bank.

The world's energy is fed by the energy that every human being and, more importantly, every couple does, because couples multiply it by two.

Positive energy exists in work that makes us struggle but not suffer; struggling is part of teaching here, suffering is part of negative energy. If you choose the world of positive energy, then you are choosing to increase your energy gradually, meaning you won't become a millionaire from one day to the next. You won't achieve your dreams overnight. You will have to work at them. How long and how hard? It really all depends on how much negativity you have created; every negative action requires 2 positive actions to outweigh it. So, if you created 2 years of negativity, you will need 4 to start seeing your life flourish.

Success is reached at 3 different levels.

Love, health, and wealth. Only a small percentage of people in the world have achieved all 3 properly. If you have too much of one, you will leave the other one unattended. You need to balance your priorities and set your energy and time in a balanced distribution. When one of the three is struggling, it's because you are not generating enough energy and attention on the other topic.

A lot of people tend to categorize those whom they see in fame as successful. But remember, you don't know what goes on behind closed doors. Focus on you.

In today's century, more than ever, it's important to find a balance between ourselves and what surrounds us. The world we see and the one we don't see. We are constantly trying to find answers outside when we know the answers we are seeking are within us. We need to find a balance between the spiritual world and the material world. Put priority on us over things.

How much time in your life do you spend paying attention to something that is making you less connected to yourself? Has your happiness become dependent on something material? If you can go a whole day without anything other than your own company and be at peace, you are connected and balanced.

It's important to be in touch with who we are as spiritual beings because the more we sink into the rabbit hole of having, it's never enough. We are beings of light, and our purpose is not to generate material wealth but a spiritual one.

Practice simplicity, where you can remotely travel to a space with as little as possible and revalue yourself as a person, connect with nature, disconnect from technology, and pay attention to the little things in life. We get so used to having what we have that sometimes we forget to appreciate and be grateful.

Being grateful is one of the most important emotions you can have; it's a sense of humility.

This is what will help you jump/progress even faster. Most people have a horrible habit of constantly complaining about the things that are not going well for them, only to generate that same energy for themselves. Energy generated by complaining doesn't reinforce what you want. On the contrary, you are generating an energy of discomfort that the universe and your body understand as ungrateful. This is an energy that will make you stagnant.

The universe doesn't understand your complaints, and your subconscious doesn't understand them either. So, whenever you say I don't want this, you are really saying I want this because you are providing and feeding that thought energy. The universe works with and understands vibration only, not words. So, what you say must always be vibrating on the line of abundance and gratitude to get the best result out of it.

Next time you find yourself complaining about something, become aware and immediately change your thought pattern to "thank you".

Karma

Our sweet old karma... To think that so many people don't believe in it. Well, I can assure you and bet my life on it that it's real. In fact, I have fun removing this from people, one of my gifts. Can you remove karma from your life? Absolutely. For every negative action, you need double the positive one to balance it out.

Every bad action you have ever taken, even if you are unaware that it was negative, will be with you eternally, literally. The energy you create is something that is marked in the ether, a signal that cannot be erased. The moment you create negative energy; you open the doors to energies. Just like time doesn't really exist, it is possible to travel to the past as it is to travel to the future, but something must be replacing that action.

This simply means you can replace the energy you created at a time by replacing it with positive energy. How can you do this? Sorry, you need 27 meditators to do so.

But what if I told you that every negative action you create deposits its negative energy inside your body? These spheres of energy are the ones that are capable of being removed by someone with strong positive energy. Removing the negativity that is tied to the negative actions or mistakes allows the person to have a second chance. It doesn't make the mistake go away, but it removes the consequence absorbed by it. Depending on how bad the situation is, of course, everything always comes around.

If there is a perfect justice system in the universe, it's definitely karma. I don't know why people go out of their way to sue others. If someone did you wrong, you can have faith in the universe that what goes around comes around. Karma is like this baggage you are carrying, and the more mistakes you make, the heavier it gets until life in general just feels heavy altogether.

You wonder why things happen to you, yet just because you feel you are a good person doesn't necessarily mean you are a good person. If you can really evaluate your life and say you have never cheated, lied, stolen, misguided, faked, used, or abused anyone in your life, then maybe you are free of karma. But most people think they are good, and they don't really evaluate their lifelong choices. It's a lot of them, over a long time.

So, if you are balancing out the years you might have generated some kind of negativity, keep in mind, regret is the most important purge of karma. The problem is that if you don't really feel sorry for what you did, to yourself maybe or others. We are talking about the smallest action, as simple as drinking too much, putting toxins down your vessel, and not taking care of your body. These are the regrets that will help you heal.

Angels & Demons

Anyone that thinks that we are the only intelligent species in this universe is just ... behind millions of years.

Just like we live in one dimension, there are unlimited amounts of dimensions and frequencies within those dimensions. There are ranges in energy when it comes to entities, and angels, or orbs, or aliens. The reality is they are all the same; they are energy manifested in different ways, existing in different vibrations, occupying a different space. We exist in one dimension or more at a time. When we sleep, we connect to other dimensions. If you have never tried REM sleep, I highly recommend it. Simply put an alarm an hour or half an hour before your wake-up call. Turn it off and go back to sleep. This will be the moment where your subconscious and conscious mind latches together, so you have a better chance of remembering what you are seeing and receive any messages you might be needing.

We have the ability to communicate outside of our visual reality. Your vision is just you tapping into what exists in this physical reality. You can talk to loved ones who have passed away in your dreams, have full-on conversations if you want. You can travel in other worlds and experience powers you don't hold in your reality. The beauty of dreams is that they will always tell you something; you just need to learn to interpret them and believe in them.

For someone who has invited negative entities into their home, the situation can unravel in the following ways... You obviously didn't know you were creating negativity because no one told you. Any act of lust, hate, anger, or depression that happens in your life is an act of weakening your positive energy and leaving a door open for negative energy to enter. If you have attracted enough negativity into your life, you will more than likely have symptoms of depression, loneliness, suicidal thoughts, aggression, etc. These kinds of entities will attract more negative entities, so you keep losing track of your path. You will suffer consequences of insomnia, nightmares, sweaty dreams like you are fighting something, and even sleep rape. The highest possession of an entity in someone is energetic rape. This is the final straw; this is a fully possessed human being without the power or say over their actions. Yes, it's real, yes, it happens, more than you think.

Victims of energy abuse sexually very rarely come forward to get help because they are just labeled as crazy, and that it's all in their imagination. There is nothing more destructive than going through something like this and not being able to tell anyone. These are extreme cases and usually happen in houses that are very charged negatively, locations near cemeteries, places where there are portals, where witchcraft has been done, or where crimes have been committed, are all possible locations to carry demons of this strength.

The second and most popular kind of negativity is the one that everyone has but can still live a relatively normal but stressful life. This negativity is the one created at home by meaningless fights, lack of love, aggression in sex, porn, substances, domestic violence...you get the idea. Sex being the most active generator, it will be the highest in energy, so any aggression will peak amounts of negativity. Substances or aggression will attract energies that are vibrating in that same tune. Most people have opened to negativity through sex and didn't even know it. Sex that is fed by lust, which is emptiness, is a physical urge that overpowers you, and you give in to it like animals; they mate for instinct. If you ever feel you have given in to the thought of aggression, where pain or mistreatment gives you pleasure, then you are an open channel for negative energy to flow into.

Even if you don't want to believe there is something evil that haunts us, just with common sense, think, what kind of energy will an aggressive action attract? It can't possibly attract a loving angel to come solve your problems. It will attract something that feeds off that exact energy that you are generating.

Negative energy absorbs your good energy and empties you out; positive energy fills your energy more, makes you feel stronger, fills your battery with light and possibilities.

People who are suffering from any type of addiction go through the process of purging their body from that addiction, but what they never think of doing is clearing their energy from all the energy they absorbed while being in the addiction, so they always go back to the same path and relapse. You can't clean the body and not clean the soul. Although your decisions are your own, we are constantly being pressured by dark energy since it's the one that's being generated the most.

We are constantly being guided; the problem is that we don't listen all of the time, and some people forget they have the ability to listen at all. We all have guardian angels, loved ones who still look out for us, and other types of energies that either push us or pull us. My guardian angel's last job was me, so he could advance to the next category of light I suppose…I think he had a very busy time keeping me alive, but he got me to where I needed to be. So if you ever hear a little voice in your head that sounds just like your thoughts, listen.

You can connect with past loved ones if you really want to. These aren't gifts for some people. These are lines of communication between us and the ether. You can tap into them whenever you want, especially in your dreams, because that is where your conscious mind will not distract you. Our messages will usually come through our dreams if we are not so connected during the day. Depending on your activities, your brain has to be available to communicate; if you are constantly processing thoughts of reasoning, you don't allow intuition to have a say.

Have you ever been in a situation where a tragedy happened, and you just so happened to run late that day? Or something within those lines. We are constantly being sent signals that we do pick up on, but we are unaware of. Becoming aware of them will just make you more sensitive to receiving them with time and just listen to the universe a little more often. Listen to your gut as if it were you speaking to you, because it's your higher self, the one you have suppressed with so much going on in your head and material life.

I think we've been so separated from listening to our thoughts and feelings because we'd rather be "entertained". Energies also have their hierarchy, according to time of existence, experience, missions concluded, etc. We can have conversations with them if we want to. You can have an intention of communicating with a specific person who has crossed over, so you just think of the person, call them, summon them. They will decide if they will accept the invitation and connect with you, if the request is pure. This usually happens in dreams. At first, you will feel a little delusional because it will feel like you are talking to yourself, until later, when you are sure you are not. Allowing ourselves to have that time and space in our minds where nothing else is forcing us to think of something as very necessary for our evolution as spiritual beings.

We attract what we are, what we carry. So, if we carry sorrow, grudges, hate, envy, lies, anger, promiscuity, what do we suppose we are going to attract? Someone with the same vibrational levels, because at the end of the day, we are just channels connecting on a larger scale.

What I can tell you about demons is that you attract them to you according to your actions. They do stay there if you don't remove them before passing, because they are energy; therefore, they cling to your energy with the ability to prevent your soul from moving on. If you have opened the door to strong negative energy and are thinking and acting on changing your life's course, it will do anything in its power to not allow you to move on because it feels it has a right over your soul since you invited it in. So yes, it's recommendable you deal with your personal issues while you are still alive rather than afterwards. This isn't a belief; this is a reality. Whether you'd like to accept it or not, 80% of our population has these parasitic beings inside of them, manipulating their everyday lives, and they don't even know it.

Suicide is the worst decision anyone could make. I apologize because what I am about to tell you will hurt some feelings, as I know family members wish their loved ones were at peace. When a person is suicidal, they are on their very last drop of energy. What pushes them over the edge is not their emotional level; it's the entities they have attracted over the past years, before reaching the final stage. This doesn't happen overnight, and because these lives are shortened before their time and with a possession of negativity, these souls are trapped by negativity, eternally, unless someone helps them clear their souls of the negative energy that traps them. This is something I know deeply because it's one of my favorite works, releasing souls that are trapped. It's incredibly fulfilling to feel so much suffering and then so much peace and gratitude afterwards. So if you are someone who has lost a loved one to suicide, don't leave them unattended and find someone who can help their soul move on.

The difference between angels and demons is that angels allow free will and demons don't. Positive energy is something you seek and need to create; negative energy is something that will be sneaking in if you allow it at a vulnerable state. We are in a silent battle between good and evil, but only if you don't want to see it, then you won't see it. Sometimes denial is a good protection towards energies.

Just be vigilant of thoughts that aren't yours, give a hand and a smile to those you can, and always try to be as pure as possible so your process here is guided by light and not sunk by darkness.

Understanding Energy

Energy is generated in many different frequencies, so it's important to know if we are covering all the spaces necessary to live an abundant life.

Every thought you have creates a frequency in energy, every emotion, and every physical action. They go by strength since thought comes before emotion and action. The stronger the thought, the stronger the energy being given to that thought. Your aura, if you might call it this, the protective layer of energy around you, must be as pristine as possible for no negativity to filter in. This means you must generate energy in every frequency available to be able to fill the space that completes this protective shield.

So, you might be thinking, I do everything right, I'm a good person, yet bad things still happen to me... why? We must dig deeply into finding how much and how often or how little you are doing something that's affecting that shield. For example, "I'm a good person." How many times a day do you judge or criticize another person? How often do you get angry at things? Do you take care of your body and what you consume? Most importantly, how often do you generate negative energy sexually with non-meaningful encounters? Most people don't even take sex into consideration when it comes to spirituality. The truth is: sex is spirituality.

There can be so many questions to go over that will help you analyze where your positivity is leaking. Let's cover the energy of sexual energy: In a relationship, it's the same reaction as on your own, just multiplied by two. If you are generating energy of love during intercourse, that's one level of energy, the strongest one, because it's the unity of two energies merging. But what if you aren't generating any energy in the sense of being there for the person, caring, loving, hugging, kissing, aiding their needs? All these actions generate a lower strength in energy, but when you add them all up, they almost take up the space of intercourse in the amount of energy they add up to. So what I am trying to have you understand is that you might be doing so many things right to your knowledge, but the little things that maybe you don't see as important are the ones leaving that weak space for negative energy to invade and affect you from something as simple as an insignificant fight, to getting fired from your job. If you are single, you need to simply reserve your sexual energy for yourself and not waste it. Although, of course, we must keep in mind that not everything that we see as bad is bad. Sometimes we expect things that we have planned out that aren't necessarily what the universe wants us to experience. We must be open and thankful for change.

Life is about moving. When there is nothing else in this world for you to move in, you will no longer exist in this reality; it's simply pointless. We are here to grow and for our souls to enrich themselves with experiences that make us vibrate higher. This is your purpose here. Shine your light and leave a path for those who come after to keep shining and continue in your evolution. Earth is just a school where we come to learn. Once we pass all its teachings, we no longer need to come back. Evolution never stops.

All negativity needs is a small spark of darkness to unravel a lot more of it. It might seem complicated but once you start to train your mind to be aware of your thoughts and actions the more it will happen naturally. It all begins with intention.

Something that happens often and is seen as insignificant is couples making love but thinking or fantasizing about another person, or worse, remembering past relationships as flashes. This is one of the causes of negativity ignitions in relationships that goes unseen. Exchange of energy at such a deep level requires all of your attention. But when you have already linked emotional affairs elsewhere, an invisible thread is created, and it will make sure to reappear the moment you are ready to settle into a positive relationship. It's a way of confusing you, and even worse when you grasp the thought and re-live it, meaning you are bringing it back to life. So, if you are meant to have pure thoughts to generate positive energy of love when you are making love, any negativity from the past will indeed come back to try to swerve you from the right path. This is when intelligence jumps in.

Energy is generated 100% by intention. So, if your intention is physically with your partner, but your mind, which is what guides the energy, is thinking of someone else, you will immediately spark a peak of negative energy at the moment that happens through your encounter. This can be reflected afterwards when you are either in a bad mood for no reason or a silly fight starts with insignificant foundations. It's different if it's a fantasy that you have spoken about with your partner before and has never happened, because there is no past action to relive or spark; you are creating it with your partner at the present time.

The best way to manage energy in your life is by awareness. You know what's right or wrong, you know what you should be doing or not doing, so you know when you are having sneaky or deviant intentions that need to be simply corrected by your own thought process. Let's think of negative energy like a virus on our computer system that needs purging and checking every day. Your mind is your CPU, you open hundreds of tabs a day, filter only the ones that benefit you, everything else, send it to the trash.

Energy is consciousness, so you need to speak to it and yourself when something comes to mind that you know should not be there, simply by ignoring the thought, squinting your eyes, shaking your head, tell it to literally go away, and reorder your thoughts. "I do not welcome these thoughts into my energy field; I live in the present and create in the present". This is where you take control of your thoughts first. It might sound silly, but it makes all the difference.

When a person comes across your path and is filled with anger and frustration and is trying to get through to you with these emotions, your reaction will change if you look at them simply not being themselves. Instead of thinking, what a crazy person, think: poor soul, it's covered in darkness, and you will learn to feel compassion for them instead of hate. Each person acting out in a form of rage or anger is fueled by negativity that they have attracted somehow, so speaking to them is facing their dark energies. Allowing their negativity to stick to yours will just prove they broke you and beat you; now it's spread like a virus that you allowed in. I take it like a game; it makes it so much more exciting. When someone tries to anger you, it's because that person's dark energy is trying to influence you, so you simply must not go along with it and see who's stronger. Should anyone really have that kind of power over you? Where they affect your state of emotions, and you lose it. This is you losing, this is when pride comes in handy. Anytime you can't control yourself to act in a state of peace, you are losing the game. The game is to be centered, peaceful, and in control as much as you can in your life, so it can lead you to smart decisions. Feel free to give yourself awards for your progress, because there is nothing more complex than the human brain, and you will try to eventually control it to the fullest.

Having control of your mind is having control of most things that happen to you. Putting aside people's mistakes that affect you of course, that we can't control.

To safeguard your aura and maintain a positive energy field, it is essential to cultivate mindfulness in every aspect of your life. By recognizing the sources of negative energy, whether they stem from thoughts, actions, or interactions, you can prevent them from infiltrating your protective shield. Consider every encounter, every word spoken, and every thought generated as a potential contribution to your overall energy balance.

Achieving this level of awareness requires diligent self-reflection and a commitment to purity of intention. Observe your daily interactions and identify moments where negativity may sneak in. Challenge yourself to correct these lapses and replace them with positive, constructive behaviors. This transformative process will not only enhance your personal energy but will also influence those around you, creating a ripple effect of positivity.

Embrace this journey as a continuous practice in your quest for emotional and spiritual growth. With patience and persistence, you will nurture a resilient and vibrant aura that repels negativity and attracts harmony and peace. Remember, the power to shape your energy lies within your thoughts and actions. Choose wisely, act compassionately, and let your inner light shine brightly. It might seem overwhelming to think you have to analyze yourself daily, but once you start your mind commands and practices it will end up happening naturally without you even noticing or putting much effort into it.

Let's dig deeper into intimacy, as it's the highest generator of energy for humans. I believe and have proven that by having control of your sexual energy, you can easily control anything else much faster and more efficiently. If you have control of your mind under the circumstances of arousal, which is the highest moving energy, you will have control of it out there on a regular day basis.

Another door opener to negative energy is thinking and acting aggressively while you are intimate. This has to be how you create the strongest peaks of negative energy for your life. So, any thought of aggression towards the other person, such as that of using them for venting or causing any kind of harm, will create peaks of negativity, because you have welcomed aggression into your life, not love. Don't misunderstand, when I mention aggression, I mean you are just having sex to vent, blow some steam off, and it could be with anyone, you needing to relieve stress into the person. You should never use someone else to release your stress into you should always want to fill them with love. Stress is filled with anger, exhaustion, grudges, and laziness; you can't possibly think dumping all that in a person is a good thing. If you don't have good energy to share, don't share it at all.

Make-up sex is probably one of the most believed to be satisfying sex some couples can have, only because it's fueled by rage, so the adrenaline rush of energy is faster, but the end results are disastrous.

You need to start thinking of sex as what it is, a connection to an outlet where you are filling up with energy, so what energy are you filling up with? Is the person you are with filled with depression, sadness, guilt, shame, anger, or grudges? All this passes through your body when you decide to exchange energies. Is your energy strong enough to deal with all those emotions, or will you be overwhelmed and end up absorbing what is not yours?

Wasting Energy

How can we waste this strength in meaningless encounters? Waste away our power...

ANY negative reaction you have from the most insignificant bad mood or weakness will weaken your energy protection. So, anything bad that happens around you will take up twice as much energy for you to fix it, eventually drying out.

Doing things that don't fulfill us. It's one thing if you are doing something for passion, where it's not a job, it's a hobby that pays. Or if you are doing something only for the responsibility of belonging. How many lives do you want to have until you finally get it? Don't waste your time on things that don't enrich your soul. If you are walking around zombied out and have lost track of why you are here, you have no energy left. You forgot your purpose. Part of that purpose is what we do almost every day of our lives.

Your job is probably what takes up half of the time in your life. Why waste it doing something that doesn't make you happy? It doesn't seem wise. Sometimes we seek standards that require too much of our attention when really, how much, how big, or how many do you need? And do you need it at all? You're not meant to live to work; you're meant to work to live better. No one will make it easy for you, but if it were easy, everyone would do it, and this book would be pointless. Humans like shortcuts, and our energy has gotten weak through them. If you are smart, you will use shortcuts for optimization and not commercialization.

The next one would be to stop wasting time feeding people and situations that do not enrich you. If you are ever surrounded by someone who doesn't see your future as successful, then simply don't be around them. These are people that normally tend to feed off others' energies.

Insignificant arguments. It's very normal for our ego to kick in and think we need to make everyone think like us. No, each person will make their decisions based on the experience and information they have had. You can't change that person's experience; you can only provide them with new information so they can draw a conclusion on their own. Never try to convince someone of your ideas; it's not right to impose our thoughts on others. When someone thinks differently than you, simply accept it and agree to disagree. Every second you waste trying to push the other person's energy is a second wasted from creating positive energy for yourself. The amount of energy you waste on emotion, voice vibration, and thought into arguments that eventually will end anyway, is something you can never get back. What you can do is time it or prevent them. When was the last time you got into an argument, and how long did it last? That long is how long you have wasted. Your battery is now at 80%. Your energy is your life, so spend it wisely.

Is there something or someone in your life that does NOT provide feelings of: love, friendship, care, support, comfort? Those who drain your energy when you speak with them:

> Write it down:

Now, who's left on the list? Who provides positive energy to you?

> Write it down:

Stay with whoever is on your good list. As drastic as this sounds. If someone on your bad list is a dear family member, you will simply just limit your time with them a little more. If this is not possible, then just come to terms with understanding that they do not see things as you do; they don't feel the same way you do for certain things, and that's totally okay. You don't have to seek anyone else to understand you as long as you do. But that doesn't mean you can't tolerate others' opinions. So next time you are sitting at a table and that one person gets on your nerves, remember he or she is a test of your tolerance. How much can you handle before it breaks you and you let negativity crawl in? The best fights are won in silence.

By limiting who we spend more time with, we are motivating ourselves to feed on positive energy throughout the day. Social energy is very important. When we are surrounded by friends, loved ones, even strangers, we are generating energy; the important thing is what kind of energy is being generated in the encounter? Start protecting your energy more; it's your youth.

Another energy waste is if you're with someone that you have no feelings for due to the fear of starting again. Instead of creating good energy, which is what couples are meant for, you will be creating an energy of friction. It doesn't have to be negative, but it won't be positive. Of course, it will have more negative inclinations because it's a void. This is bad, because both of your energies will be in a state of defense, so you will be more tense, low on energy, tired, lack of proximity, and so on and so forth. This is a waste of energy. Let each person be loose to choose what is best for them. You will not get the time back, so don't waste it on what you know is not for you. The more you insist on something, the more you are trying to manipulate and shift the nature of the sequence of events. Do not insist and learn to accept. Allow yourself to be more present, but most of all, more open verbally. Express your emotions. Express your feelings, what have you been wanting to say for a long time and don't say it? Why do people waste so much money on paying someone to make you come to the sense of what you already know? You're capable of expressing what you feel at any time in the most honest way possible. So why not be able to share your feelings with the person you choose to be the most intimate with? If you want to know if your partner is right for you, or if you're paying attention? It's simple:

Are they your best friends?

Can you be at your most vulnerable state around them?

Would you trust them with your life?

Do you have no secrets?

Your partner needs to be the person who knows you the most at your best and at your worst and still love you; you should have no fear of telling them anything; they are your best friends.

More energy wasting is done worrying about the future. Probably one of the most common things to do, especially if you have responsibilities. Slowly accept that you only have real control of the present. You can only manipulate the decision-making you are doing now. You can control how you react to people, how you accept or decline invitations, jobs, and friends. You can choose to be angry, sad, upset, complain, or choose to smile, be happy, calm, and find solutions.

There is no one else to hold responsible for your life today other than yourself. Because whatever story you tell yourself, it's the cause of what you experience. Today is only enabling you to be the way you are today, meaning you accept it and take it as a reality, quit finding excuses and take responsibility.

Stressing about what could have should have and things that are out of your reach is another energy waste. Analyze the situation, and if there is absolutely nothing you can do about it, don't spend more time thinking about it. You will literally burn out energy. You will spend so much energy thinking away and never find a solution. Focus and give more time and energy to the things that can balance out the bad, the things you can control and do something about.

Waiting around for others is another big energy waste. Accepting that our transit in this space is temporary and unique. We are not tied to anyone unless we choose to; we are just all connected. Don't wait for someone to change if there is no personal intention in it; people change when they really want to and take the initiative on it. You should never force them; it's respecting free will, unless of course you need to intervene in a health issue.

Settling is one of the reasons you might not be progressing. We tend to find ourselves in comfort zones that are difficult to get out of because we are afraid of change. You find yourself steady but not progressing. You might think this is all that you deserve, but you will only be as good as what you put out to be. You deserve the best and should never settle for anything less than that. This all starts with valuing yourself first. Most of the lack of confidence we have comes from our childhood, so go back to the mental training program and do it.

Another huge waste of energy is worrying about what happens in other people's lives. There are a lot of people today who spend more time living other people's lives than their own. What would you expect to happen? Instead of taking responsibility for your life and what you want in your life, some prefer to entertain themselves to forget about responsibilities. Because it's just too complicated, too much time is invested. Value what's worth more, your life or others?

Stop wasting energy and make some choices that you know are needed.

Write down the things or people that you feel make you waste energy:

Friends

You don't have to search for friends; friends appear on their own, naturally. You cannot go to them; rather, they come from somewhere and are the compatible ones. Don't try to change the natural ways. If You haven't found any, it's because there are no compatible people around you.

In life, people can generally be grouped into four distinct categories based on their relationship with money and love. Understanding these types can help you recognize which relationships are beneficial and which may drain your energy or hinder your personal growth.

1. Those Who Have Neither Money nor Love

Individuals in this group often lead lives filled with resentment and disbelief. They feel lost, constantly searching for something that seems out of reach. Their outlook may be negative, and their energy can impact those around them. It is advisable to maintain distance from them, as their perspective can be draining and may prevent you from moving forward positively.

2. Those Who Have Money but No Love

People who possess wealth but lack love tend to feel powerful and self-assured. However, this confidence can manifest as arrogance; they may believe they know everything and are frequently argumentative, always seeking to prove themselves right. Engaging with them is often unproductive and can waste your time and energy.

3. Those Who Have No Money but Have Love

This group is characterized by hopefulness and a sense of well-being. They maintain a positive attitude and are optimistic about their future progress. Their upbeat nature often attracts many friends, and interacting with them is generally enjoyable. They can be a source of inspiration and genuine connection.

4. Those Who Have Both Money and Love

People in this category are typically happy and enterprising. They listen attentively and show respect for others' opinions. Their balanced approach to life makes them desirable companions and role models, contributing positively to those around them.

Relationships

You can't possibly expect to attract the right person to you if you are not vibrating according to your expectations. Also, what are those expectations? Are you looking to find someone to care about you, or are you looking for someone to look good on your Instagram page? Today's main issue is shallowness and shields. The subliminal messaging that the entertainment industry has put out has changed what most people are seeking in a partner; the importance is appearance before value. There is this picture-perfect image of what a couple should look like.

First stop trying to show yourself as a perfect match, that never works out. You don't want to attract someone just because you look good and act; accordingly, you want to attract someone who sees past your looks. So, being relaxed, carefree, and natural is the best way to go if you are hoping to find love forever. Taking so much time to look good at the gym or at the salon so you can be attractive to others will only attract exactly that. People who are only interested in your looks and a temporary good time.

I can tell you thousands of people run into their soulmates in their life and never realize it. Most people dismiss their soul mate without knowing because they don't even give them a chance. They simply didn't meet their expectations. Being so busy making sure the list of requirements is checked at every box that they forget about the most important thing, which is chemistry. We have grown apart from self and given matter more worth.

If you are someone who lacks confidence and self-love, you will be vibrating at a level of frequency that will attract another person at the same level of vibration. Two low vibrating beings can come together but will only flourish if they are working together to be better and vibrate higher. If there is no mutual work to be better, then you will simply stay stuck within that same frequency and eventually lower. This is why it's so important to first focus on healing yourself and becoming the best version of yourself. Or find someone who will walk the path with you in improvement. Relationships are meant to multiply and progress together.

Our energy is based on our emotional level. So, the more emotions you have that weigh on the negative side, the more they will attract you to situations and people that are more on that side, and vice versa. We are constantly attracting people into our lives; the key is to know how to attract the right ones.

The only way of doing this is to stop looking for someone to complete you and look within instead. Evaluate the key points you need to work on, starting with the triggers that cause you to have certain emotions that push people away. Jealousy, envy, rage, depression, possessiveness, insecurity. Get rid of those triggers first, become aware of when you are having these emotions, so you can identify them and control them, eventually leaving them behind.

Finding the perfect match means you have found the perfect chemistry. Your body, mind, and spirit need to be in tune. To know if your bodies are compatible, you will feel very comfortable with the person's chemical release, their skin, sweat, and odor. When you are with someone and there is no chemistry, you will find unpleasant smells that are basically your body negatively reacting to the person; of course, there are always exceptions. Your spirit will know if it's the energy that completes it by a simple gut intuition, but this gut intuition should only be followed if you have already healed. You can't follow your instincts if you are toxic and filled with negative energy; it will only lure you towards wrong intuition. The mind is the most difficult to convince, always put the first two first, allowing your mind to be open to the possibility of a match with chemistry and spirit.

Sometimes people tend to put so much effort into finding the right person that they forget to find themselves first. If you can't find yourself, then what hope do you have to find a perfect match? Things will happen when the time is right and you are ready.

When we get involved with someone who is problematic or toxic, it's entirely our fault because we put ourselves in that situation; we attracted that toxic relationship without even knowing. Without a proper evaluation of how you are doing internally, you will never understand why it is you keep falling into the same patterns. These people aren't just falling on your path due to bad luck; you are causing these attractions.

Some people hope for a relationship to fill a void of loneliness, but all that time, you could be working on a better version of yourself so you can attract a better version of a partner. Clearing our energy is crucial so that we can go about our lives without negative influences causing negative patterns.

If you are going through depression, you are not necessarily going to attract someone also going through depression, but you will attract someone vibrating within similar parameters as your depression. It's why we feel so comforted by people going through similar cases as ours. This way, we feel comforted, warm, and safe. Humans will always try to seek comfort because otherwise they must face their demons, and we can safely say not everyone is ready to do this.

When we go through moments of heartbreak, our energy gets hurt, but it also creates a stronger comeback if we know how to view the situation. If someone decides you are no longer good enough for them because there is no match, then embrace this by thanking the universe for making them realize sooner than later. Because what good is it if you are in a relationship where the feelings are not reciprocal, and it will inevitably end at some point anyway. Crying over what could have been a waste of energy that you could be focusing on getting back on track for better opportunities.

It's very important to get to know the person before you decide if they are meant for you, and when I mean to get to know them, I mean their past, how many people they have been with before their 20's. Why would you be ashamed of asking these things? It's important to know everything you possibly can about the person's sexual habits because, according to that, it is how much you will have to work on healing and also you need to find someone compatible with what your body needs. If you were promiscuous in your teens, you would suffer from marrying someone who is very passive sexually.

If there is chemistry and you feel they are your match, know the facts beforehand so you go into the relationship with this knowledge and can surpass any complications when they appear, because after finishing this book, you know they will appear. It's better to be aware of and ready for them than be blinded. Where there is love, everything can heal.

Every person we cross tracks with has something to teach us, and we have something to teach them. Learning to accept this and not deny ourselves from actual situations will save us a lot of time and trouble. The key points are time that you can't get back, and vulnerability that attracts negativity, which you will later have to work twice to get rid of. So, looking into the future with an open heart and mind will ensure you attract better outcomes.

Things don't end from one day to the next; they build up until they fall apart. At some point or another, you lose track, so know that the future will inevitably be better than the past because, unless you mess up in some way, the universe will reward you for your growth. Always say thank you for the positive moments and regret the bad ones, so you can purge yourself from them and leave them behind. Lots of people are against regret, but I can guarantee you it's the most effective purge you can do to remove negativity from your life, regretting moments that generate bad energy for your life.

Negativity will always be lurking to find a way in when you find the right person. This is when all the mental programming helps the most because you learn to be aware of when thoughts aren't yours or you are having reactions that do not go with your principles. Always have an open heart and make decisions in love based on your gut feeling and instinct.

You are meant to be able to meet your expectations in life. This means you still need to be able to accomplish your dreams, and a good partner will always support your dreams because they will want to see you happy and accomplished in your projects.

The Shield

This is one of the most suffered, unknown conditions in the world today for women, which affects all men and society. A shield is a loss of pleasure in life. This topic has helped heal a lot of relationships, and I hope it nourishes you as well. I know that if younger generations know that they lose their chance of success in life by sleeping around, most, if not all of them, will take different measures into the promiscuity that exists today. Something that haunts millions of homes and marriages.

The shield is something that's generated within a woman's body when she loses sensitive spots. It's the lack of sensitivity. We call it a shield because it can be felt as a shield of feelings, meaning you have an actual shield covering your heart and making you cold as a person. Without the real feelings of love, you become incapable of feeling real love.

It's mainly known to women because women are more vulnerable and open at the time of intimacy, they have a higher risk of wear and tear. Women who have a shield are always falling into a ripple of attracting the same kind of men, feeling unloved, getting bored with someone after a few months, the right man might cross her path, and she won't see it because he is not up to her social standards. Women who don't have shields are not shallow; they see through the physical shell and fall in love with the right soul mate. Another aspect of a shield is a woman who takes a long time to feel arousal or finds herself with pain during intercourse or needs long and aggressive movements to feel anything at all. The loss of sensitivity is something that will create a void that needs to be filled with something more physical, this is normally when external things start to play a role in relationships, like the need for toys or another person or videos, etc. The loss of sensitivity is cut wires to the ether, so your connection when activating your sexual energy will take a little longer, and will be influenced by negative frequencies, so you don't make it to an aroused state quickly, meaning your connection is jammed or dimmed.

It's almost as if when we are aroused, we are elevating our souls to the ether, and by having a shield, the karma attached to that shield stops us from elevating.

The problem with shields is that, usually in relationships, this isn't something known or talked about. So, it leads husbands to feel like they are no longer enough to arouse their woman, making them feel less as men and hurting their self-esteem. Sex is an act to be taken in a two-way pleasure, if one person feels like doing it is a "job" because their partner doesn't feel, this will eventually lead to a slow but steady distance in sexual encounters, hurting the whole relationship overall. Women with shields will always find an excuse not to have intimacy because the negativity they carry stops them from bettering themselves by creating positive energy in the strongest way.

This is when intelligence plays a role. If you are intelligent enough to see these reactions as a way of negative energy stopping you from growing, you will fight against those thoughts and put more effort into feeling pleasure.

If your highest way of generating energy is not being exercised, what energy are you left with? Good thoughts, positive affirmations, and actions? These are simply not enough to push you towards success. Your sexual energy generation is the highest energy you can create with another person. Humans are made to perfection; each genitalia work like a key, there is someone in the world for each of us, who fits perfectly like a key when the two bodies connect. Can you believe there is someone in this world cut perfectly to fit the rings of your genitals? Well, yes.

The shield is something that we have proven is treatable, after 10 years of studying it and removing it with positive energy, which does have the power to clear it and awaken new sensitive spots, replacing the ones that were cut. You can't reawaken sensitive spots that have been cut off, but you can open new ones. There must be love of healing from the male to the female to be able to reawaken the body. This is where the patience, caring, and love of a partner come in. When a man loves a woman enough to want her to flourish, he will dedicate his time to reopening the woman's channel and sensitivity. This takes time, but with affection. It's the energy generated by the love of time and dedication that will spark new spots back up. When the pleasure points are all awakened, both in man and woman, and the chemistry is right, their bodies will have a chemical and energetical reaction to each other being close and far away. The connection you create when both channels are awakened is indescribable. Your body will release fluids through currents of pleasure throughout the day when talking or thinking about that person. You finish each other's sentences, you feel what the other person needs, you are in constant connection with their energy, and you are now a source of energy completing a full circle.

That's really what your other half means; it means the energy that will bind your energy into a circle of infinity. Just like the Ying and yang, man and woman were created to bring life to this planet and to create vessels for souls to grow in and learn.

Unfortunately, women who have shields will tend to make more mistakes than those who don't because they cannot and should not trust their instinct, which will lead them to wrong decisions. It will make them be shallower and choose men by society's norms, not by their chemistry. They will feel like they are in love for the first 3 months and then that love is confused by lust and they stay in a vicious cycle. Women with shields will always have a headache or an excuse. They are normally going through dryness, and if the case is very strong, they even smell of messed-up chemistry inside their body. They will have more inclination to be unfaithful. In some cases, even disassociated with any physical touch within relationships. It's what most men call "penguins".

Women with shields also generate mostly negative energy because the lack of sensitivity weakens their connection. So, negative energy can crawl in, and this unfortunately fills the ether with bad energy. It's why it's so important for women and men to understand the need to recover their sensitivity. I think it's better to know this information even if it hurts some, so action is taken and lives are changed.

The shield will block sensitive spots from all over your body, so if there is any sexual act that you reject and see as incorrect, those are exactly the ones you need to work on the most. For example, not wanting to do oral sex to your partner = loss of sensitive spots on your mouth (produced from kissing and negative energy). We will discuss this further on. Any type of sexual trauma you feel you have because of a bad experience will be exactly the trauma you need to heal. Think of it like this: if you love your partner, there isn't any sexual act you wouldn't want to experience with them because you love them and any act would be a feeling of pleasure, if everything is done with love.

If this resonates with you or your partner, the first step to healing is acknowledging you didn't make these mistakes knowingly. But now that you know, you must work on it. This is a blockage that you can have for the rest of your life if you don't work on it.

If we can heal our future generations by preventing them from making the same mistakes, we might just have a chance for a brighter future. The world is meant to live in pleasure; it's a pleasure to be alive.

How do I know if I have a shield?

Y	N

1. You take a long time to get aroused
2. You always attract "bad individuals"
3. You like the rush, not the stability
4. You are always looking for something new
5. You can't settle down
6. Your relationships don't last
7. You're stuck
8. You hate certain sexual acts with your partner
9. You don't like body fluids from your partner

Remembering what it was like to have a shield, I can recommend several things:

1. It's probably not them, it's you.
2. First, analyze yourself to see how critical a state your shield is in
3. Work on healing yourself before you involve someone else into your life
4. You want to attract someone when your energy is positive
5. If you are already with someone, make sure they are also on a healing path to support you in the process as well. Don't get involved with people who have no intention of evolving.

6. Don't confuse lust emotions and love emotions
7. Take your time when sharing yourself sexually with someone; you don't need another disappointment
8. Don't let go of something good because you don't feel butterflies; remember, you lost these. Decide when you are healed.
9. Train your body to open new sensitive spots again and feel love again
10. Persevere
11. Never give in to negativity

If you don't like to do oral sex, your mouth sensitivity is gone. If you don't like your partner releasing on your body or face, it's a gland that the body has that makes you feel pleasure when ejaculation is on the body; it's probably dormant, too. Any loss of sensitivity is the shield.

Meditators:

Consequences that every woman is suffering who has this situation of the shield. (Woman mainly because they are the ones to suffer from shields the most)

1 - Periodically, the woman suffers from decompensation, or undefined discomfort, or anxiety without knowing why, or sometimes spontaneous headaches, or

discomfort where she is. She cannot define what she has, and it is not a disease that can be fought medically. It is that she needs a change of skin, she needs another human body acid, she needs a different vaginal pumping, she needs to satisfy that hidden addiction that the body possesses.

2 - For the woman to achieve orgasm, it always needs to come from her clitoral region. That is, a woman with a shield cannot have an orgasm from simple pumping in a few seconds, so she needs to touch herself or be touched on her clitoris, which means masturbating or being masturbated while being pumped. To be clearer, it makes the husband or partner must masturbate the woman to be able to please her while simultaneously pumping her vagina, its unnatural. masturbation occurs through simple bodily friction in the clitoral region, that is, achieving a pumping movement while the skin is rubbing against each other's clitoral.

The woman with armor loses the natural condition for which intimate relations were conceived. It is similar in humans or animals; it is always done through simple vaginal friction and not through the addition of masturbation.

3 - Periodic saturation, sometimes every few years, with the person by her side,

annoyance at listening to them, at their opinions, at their tone of voice, saturation, a feeling of being ordered around and not cared for, a need to distance herself temporarily, and this is due to the loss of values.

The armor (shield) generates an absolute loss of values and, many times, even respect, by not valuing what is by her side.

    All these items, our doctor friend and we too, believe, can be partially overcome through Positive Energy. One can learn to feel love, desire, a need for constant coexistence, and appreciation for the person. Positive Energy could reverse this bothersome and harmful situation for couples who are compatible with each other. It would be a beginning to live with fullness

Meditation

Meditation, according to my group of 27 nomad meditators, is usually not done correctly. They have taught me that if you aren't putting a purpose on meditation, then you are wasting time. Many people think that by just allowing their minds to go blank is enough for them to have a more spiritual life.

The reality is that since every moment of your life, you are generating energy, meditating on a void just creates that, a void. So, you aren't generating positive or negative energy, you are just relaxing enough for your mind to wander and connect to other frequencies. What you weren't aware of is that there can be frequencies that literally lead you nowhere.

A lot of people spend hours of their lives meditating and feeling good afterwards. They come back from this beautiful meditation where they felt elevated and weightless. An hour went by, or maybe two, and every time they train to meditate for longer and longer. We aren't meant to be living in an energetic level only; it's why we are in this physical world. Unless you are a trained meditator, you should not be meditating for more than 30 to 40 minutes a day, max.

Life is about being in action, generating energy; this means moving, doing, creating, coming, and going. You cannot expect to progress if you don't get into action. If you sit around waiting for the universe to deliver without any energy being created, you will just lose time.

Meditation needs to have a purpose; what is your purpose before you get into this meditation? Maybe it is disconnecting after all, but if you make it a habit, it can become addictive, just like anything else. Why? Because most people who are still trying to find their path sometimes get into a mode of disconnecting to forget. Just like an alcoholic or drug addict does those negative addictions to forget about their problems, as far as this example goes, because, of course, meditating isn't bad at all. But the process of it becomes similar. Where people look to meditate so they can forget about their problems or failures in life that they must face. It's easier to disconnect from reality and connect to a reality where physical isn't needed and energy is king.

Don't get dragged into the wormhole of nothingness. Meditation can be a great tool to make you receive the answers you need and the movement of energy you need. But if you just go into it with an empty void thought, then you are not doing it right.

Something delicate that you also need to keep in mind is what you are connecting with when you meditate. There are several people who have been able to connect with other living species, energies, and believe they are getting the right information to then spread to their peers. Lots of energy can be disguised as good to give you conflicting messages.

I don't recommend meditating with the purpose of communicating with anything higher if you are not cleansed and pure. For this, you must be at a level of serenity in your life. To make sure that what you are connecting with is positive. When you enter a meditation with intentions of communication, you become a receiver antenna, and if your vibration isn't right, the wrong messages can come through disguised as good but with flawed information.

A way of knowing if you are receiving information that is from a light source is very simple. When you are perceiving the information, be present with how your gut and/or stomach feels. Go over the information after you are done and see how it makes you feel inside. Does it align with a message of purity? A positive being will never tell you what you need to do, as they respect free will. If you are getting information that seems a little too demanding, like that, you must do something, then you are simply just being manipulated. Go over the information you received several times if you have doubts. When you receive valid information from a positive source, you will immediately feel a holy type of feeling in your body where fulfillment and reassurance take over, without doubts.

So next time you decide you want to meditate, start with a simple intention. Use this time not so much to be at peace but to discover the mysteries in your mind that can help you reach the next level of consciousness. Give your mind commands and move energy towards your goals.

Email from our 27 meditators:

"Most women today suffer from a significant problem, and it is due to those sexual actions in their adolescence, as disturbing the development of sensitive points causes there to be no inner revolution of love. In other words, the invisible sensitive points are the ones that generate falling in love. So, these women attend seminars because they have two possible life paths: either they live with a companion, that is, a husband or partner, but he is nothing more than a life companion—there is no love, there is affection, and they care for him, but they are not in love—or the other way of life, which is in solitude. Both can almost be considered as women need to find the purpose of their lives; they lack love, which is essential for what we were made for—to fall in love. So They attend seminars to learn to meditate or to meditate in groups to feel accompanied and, at the same time, find a way out. Others live alone, and when they wake up each morning, they don't have that love by their side to hug and kiss and say, "I love you." The phrase "I love you" doesn't exist, and so they fill that space in two ways: either they start meditating every morning, or they find a task to do to distract themselves.

For those who live with a partner as companions, even if they are married and even have children, it's the same—they don't hug their husband or kiss him because there is no love, only companionship. It's caring for each other, but the word "love" is absent, and that woman must one day find a way out, a goal. She can be described as empty. So, they try to fill that void with meditation, with those Temescal's, with those rituals where they are promised change. They try everything, but they always end up the same. In other words, meditation seminars yield no NOTHING; it only helps cleanse negativity in **some cases,** where one knows how to meditate very deeply, but meditation is nothing more than a way to fill the voids of human beings due to a lack of love in a relationship or exciting feelings, as they are cold. Meditating is not a waste of time if it

is used for specific purposes, but if it is to fill a void, it is a complete waste of time, and it is preferable for people to find a hobby or task to do. You cannot seek to have love when the mold was broken in adolescence, but you cannot tell them that because there is nothing uglier than taking a toy away from a child. Meditation is their toy that substitutes for
People want change, they need to work with their sexual Energy, directly, sexually, to avoid beating around the bush in understanding. It's about energizing to each individual. People need to take the leap, break out of the monotony of meditation without real utility, and enter the segment of Energy to feel profound and significant changes.

-27 Meditators-

Intuition

Being blind to your power of perceiving is what makes you fall into wrong companionship or decision making. If you paid attention to your intuition a little more, you would stay clear from negativity.

As we know, the strongest energy we can absorb is always going to be sexual energy because arousal is what makes us vulnerable to energy, so learning to perceive positive videos from negative ones will save you a lot of trouble.

There are two types of connections, the one you will make towards an elevated state of consciousness and heightened feeling, and the one that will make your mind very present and focused on your physical state alone.

If you were using your perception accordingly, you would not even come close to videos or people that make you connect to negativity because you would repel it. And if you don't repel it, it's simply because you have negativity yourself, so it becomes a normal frequency which you are constantly exposed to, making negative your new normal and deceiving your perception. The more contaminated you are with negative energy the more you cannot trust your instinct because it will guide you the wrong way.

So, to begin, evaluate your energy levels by simply analyzing your life, your progress, and your happiness; are you stuck?

Start to make more decisions on how you feel rather than what you think you feel. Pay attention to how your overall body reacts when you are involved in something. Does your body feel relaxed and calm, does your stomach feel well, or do you feel tension?

If you are someone who enjoys watching adult films, it's crucially important to know what type of energy you are connecting with when watching them. One arousal will open you up to receive negativity and another positive or neutral and nothing at all. To begin with, the acts on a video generate the same type of energy you would in real life. So, if in a video you are watching there is aggression, you will connect to aggressive thoughts which will then attract negative energy. If the video is normal or gentle, you will have gentle thoughts and therefore generate neutral or positive energy. You can really tell if you decide to release it, analyzing the next day how your day went. This will show you if you just wasted energy you needed, cleansed, or created good energy for progress.

If you connected to negativity, you would probably need more of it because negativity is addictive. It will make you feel like it's not enough until you end up watching more hardcore videos and it will affect your everyday life. You will slowly run out of your own energy and feel depressed or empty inside just needing to feed that need of physical pleasure. Every time you will be less connected to your energetic self and lose touch with your sensitive side.

If you are connected to something neutral, it won't have much of an effect on you, it will simply be a waste of your energy, but you will not be gathering an addiction or negative reactions in your life.

If you are connected to positive energy, you will feel tired because your body will cleanse toxic energy out, but only to later feel fulfilled and relaxed. You will feel whole, focused and with strength to take on any task thrown your way. You feel confident, secure, and optimistic.

Be careful what you expose your mind and energy to; it's your most valuable asset. Always remember that being aroused is the same as your antenna receiving energy flow; it's a wonderful action as long as you don't allow toxic energy to filter into your open channel.

Open Channel

The importance of an open channel defines how successful you will be in life, especially when you unite your energy with someone else. You must be connected, not disconnected, and most of the systems made today are to aid in our disconnection. Your body is a battery that needs feeding of energy to live prosperously. If your channel is blocked, your abundance will be blocked. If you are with a partner, they will have to make twice the effort to balance out the imbalance of energy flowing through to the relationship.

There are physical ways of knowing if your channel is blocked, and they are very simple. If you can hit every note singing, your channel in your throat is well, you don't have to be in tune, but you have to be able to have sound in all possible frequencies. Try it out. Lay out a sound for every note on a keyboard, even if it's flat; it doesn't matter. We are looking for sound, not tune. The other part of your channel is your genitals. For women, if your channel is closed at the root, you will have pain, discomfort, and dryness. Depending on the severity, the more closed the channel is. For a man, it's important to be able to have an erection with no problem; if you suffer from erectile dysfunction, then your channel is blocked. Anything aside from those three points is irrelevant because if your channel is wounded at any end, you must go to physical therapy for it, literally.

With this, I mean, that any therapy you do outside of trying to heal those spots, you will not be very successful in doing.

We are beings that are meant to live in pleasure, not fear or pain. See yourself as something other than what you have been seeing until now. You are not here to just fill up space and obey others or give away half of your life for others' progress. You are here for a much bigger vision. Do not let anyone fool you into becoming just earthly.

An open channel means abundance flows through you, and when I say abundance, I don't mean millions of dollars. I mean fulfillment of love, passion, health, and wealth in a perfect balance. This is a channel that has either never closed or has healed to be able to open and channel energy at any time.

An open channel means a fluorescent tube of light that is in constant communication with the ether. Wisdom comes hand in hand with a fully opened channel; intelligence also comes hand in hand with it. Such as extremely smart individuals who have invented things to change humanity. A lot of times, they're trapped in solitude because they can't seem to fit in with the rest of society, because they simply see things differently.

Having an open channel doesn't mean you will be successful in all things. It simply means you have the connection strong enough to be able to download all the information you need, and sometimes some that you don't need, but the world needs. For some people who can't manage so much information, they can get lost in solitude with an overload of knowledge.

Having so much wisdom can become isolating, so it's important to find a balance to live a fulfilled life in all aspects. Some of the greatest minds have had open channels, and their mission was to inform society or bring innovations to the world, but usually in loneliness.

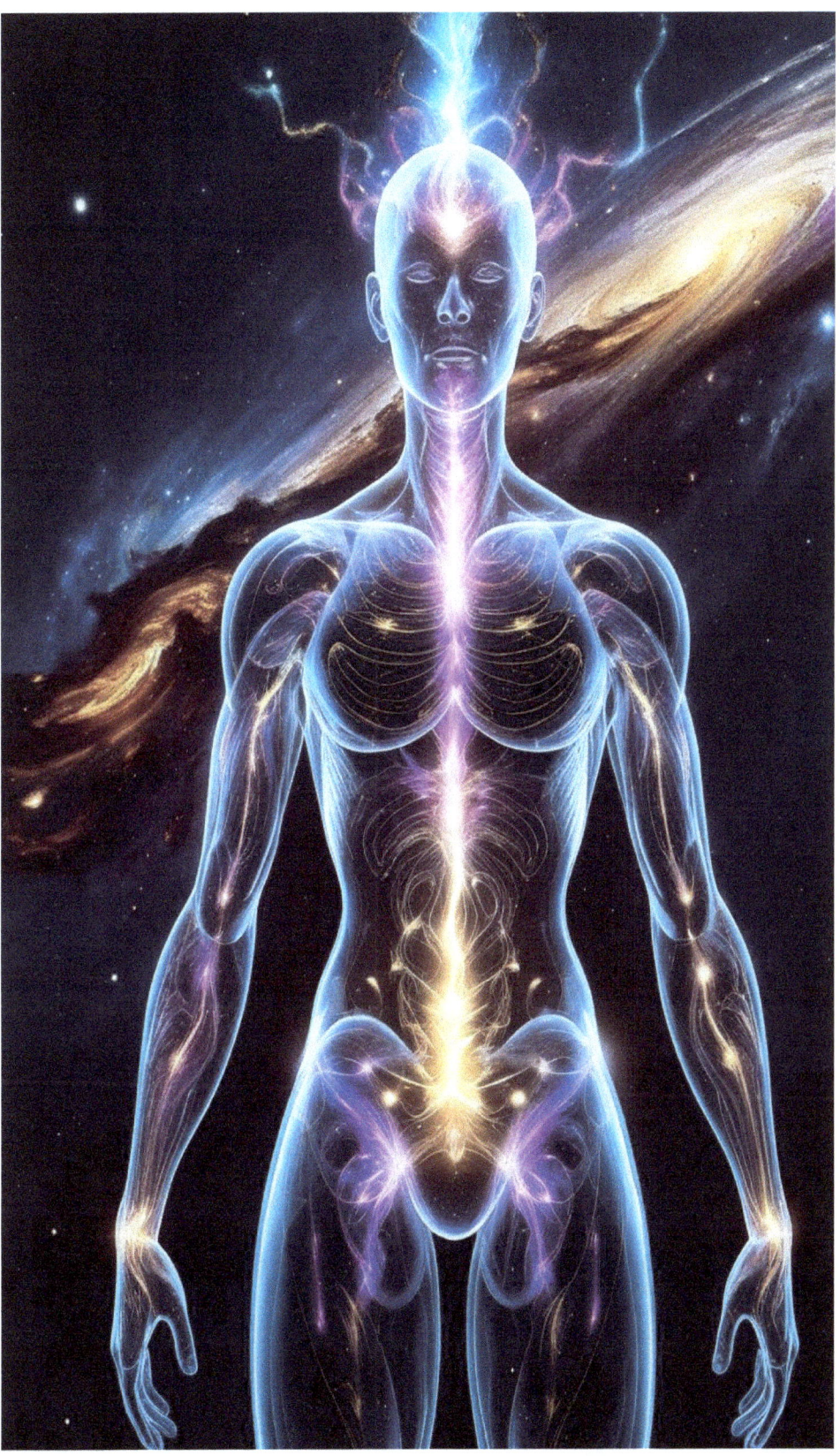

Transcending

The Only thing you need to know about death is that it's only physical. Think of it as a snake that sheds its skin; we lose our skin, and then if needed, we come back in another very similar one. The most important information about death is that you want to get there as positive as possible because negative energy is something that clings on to the soul more than the body. This means that when your body dies, the negative energy you hold inside of you will continue with your soul, not allowing you to transcend to the light. Yes, there is a light, the ether, where we come from.

So basically, the most important thing in life is to progress, grow, ascend and leave this place wiser and brighter than when we came into it. Whether it's a journey of bettering ourselves and a few people around us, or millions. Each of us has a different journey and holds a different story. By growing old without the burden of negative energy, you will then ascend faster and more smoothly.

I've had 2 NDE (near death experiences), and I love releasing trapped souls, and I can tell you the moment we leave this dimension, we feel like we are floating, alleviated of any physical pain, at ease, at peace. Our emotion of worry persists for a few human days, as time will pass differently when you are not affected by gravity, and there is no sensation of time when you are in the spiritual realm. When my father passed away, he was in touch with me the moment I entered the house where he passed and said, "It feels funny, but I no longer hold physical pain". He wouldn't stop talking to me for at least 3 months; it drove me a little nut, but as time went on, I realized his personality was also fading slowly away. He was becoming more ethereal, wiser, and holier until his voice became close enough to mimic the energy itself. It became quieter and less communicative up until now, and he only comes forward when I call for him, but I just know he is there.

      In the first moments of your passing, you will feel as if you're being lifted away from your body, flying upwards, and you will have millions of emotions rushing through, mainly the shock of vertigo that will last seconds because you are no longer in your body. Anything that made you human will slowly start to shed. A few hours after, you will have undergone an explosion of Pandora's box where everything you thought you did right may be somewhere wrong, you see your personality from a different perspective, you see your surrounding relatives with a different perspective, without the judgment of what society had made you think. If you did wrong by someone, especially those who depended on your care for growth, you will feel obligated to stay and help until that person is back on track. Imagine having to wait until you can't talk, express yourself, or be seen to finally have to do something about it.

Because it's not really a choice, elevating back to the ether means you must be pure again, so redemption is necessary. If you don't want to face your mistakes in physical life, you will have a much harder time in the spiritual one. So, it's better to deal with things in this realm so that your transcending is flawless.

Sexual Minds

Millions of people in the world have the mental programming of seeing sex as something sinful, ugly, degenerated, you can't talk about it, you get a bad taste just from reading this, maybe... All of this was cultivated into your mind and spread through your body as your reality. The reality you allowed others to choose for you, where you gave up your free will and never got it back since the moment you were commanded by these ideologies. If it's not a parent-planted seed, another option is some type of negative energy possession that usually happens in negative locations in open spaces of nature; it's usually the first one.

Too many women see the genital area and can't even name it without feeling embarrassed. The brainwashing about our powers has long been hidden, so we see divergence as the problem, when, in reality, divergent people are seeing reality.

Your sexual energy will be discovered the day you decide to dump all you know about sex, your body, and energy, and rewire with new experiences. Fighting against fear, shame, embarrassment, guilt, and low self-esteem. Some people will never ever put sex and spirituality in the same sentence...when the reality is, it's the most spiritual act humans can have and are doing, all wrong!

So, break free from any ideas; if you learned how to have sex through porn, throw away that programming inside your CPU, clear and delete your programming codes of what you believe sex is, what an orgasm is, what you are and are capable of. There will be no better power than the one you will receive from the healing of your sexual energy, and only you are standing in the way of that.

If there is anything that bothers you from the conversation of sex, find someone you trust whom you can let it all out to, unfiltered. Share your programmed teachings, where maybe your parents made it a prohibited word at home.

A sexual mind is not a bad mind if it's connected to positive energy. Talk about sex, get to know your body, buy yourself a toy, pamper yourself like you would the rest of your body and the most important word of all: RELAX. If you have a sex subject trauma in your head you need to break it, and unfortunately, the older you are, the more difficult it will be, so better late than never. *Instead of repressing and limiting the sensation of arousal, you will embrace it and expand it.*

You will not be ashamed of feeling and learning to prosper with positive energy. So now that your mind is open for new information about sex... here we go...

Sexual Energy

Sex is what animals have, something created by instinct. Today, humans are behaving like animals. Humans are meant to "generate energy" by making a conscious decision and redirecting the energy.

It's basically an all-in-one spiritual act and ritual. You have meditation, body flow, and voice activation. This is the highest stage of energy movement a body can manage. Start to look at your genitals as if they were engines that produce energy, the engines of creation. We have been given a gift to bring life into this world and generate positive energy to nourish the world. It takes a real spark of energy to create intelligent life, and we have it; we have control of the world through our sexual energy actions.

Everyone will have a different point of view of what sexual energy is or means. In my life and experience it's the strongest energy humans can create, explosions of energy created from our body, and emanated to the ether.

Sexual energy is just energy, the life force that we have inside of us, the force that moves us. We incarnate connected to the ether through hundreds of energy threads, also known as sensitive spots. We are born guided and protected always. These energy spots are the ones that are activated when we go through puberty, not to say that they were not activated before it's just that before we hit puberty, our energy is completely dependent on the energy of our parents. If we are born in a household where love and prosperity are what reign, that will be the example we will absorb as a foundation of who we will be in the future. It is very delicate when we are born into environments of negativity.

For example, domestic violence, alcohol, drugs and any other example you might think of that would generate negativity, sometimes as simple as a badly managed divorce. There are people who will go through divorce smoothly and remain friends, and there are others who make the situation extremely difficult to go through, leaving kids completely unprotected energy-wise. Once that shield that your parents are meant to provide for you while you are in a stage of growth is broken, you are exposed to being influenced and absorbing negativity around you. This will make an absolute difference in your teenage years because what negative energy wants you to do is get as far away from your positive life line as possible. So, kids who go through these kinds of vulnerable situations in their early years tend to be those kids who, in their teens, end up being very difficult to handle, rebellious, and just altogether finding the wrong people and places to hang out with.

You cannot have sex without creating energy; it's physically impossible. Your body's energy is moved by molecules that later on create endorphins, which are the hormones created by pleasure. These little molecules, born in the brain's pituitary gland and hypothalamus, are the body's natural painkillers. They glide through our system, latching onto opioid receptors in the brain, spinal cord, and beyond. When they connect, it is like flipping a switch—pain signals get muffled, and a wave of relief washes over you. But it is not just about dulling pain. Endorphins are mood-lifters, too, sparking feelings of euphoria, like the glow you get after a good laugh or a heartfelt hug. That is why you feel lighter after a workout or a moment of pure joy. What is wild is how their movement ties everything together. As these molecules travel, they talk to our nervous system, calming stress and even giving our immune system a nudge to stay strong. It is like they're weaving a safety net, helping us push through tough moments—whether it's a grueling hike or a stressful day. The way endorphins and other molecules flow through us, coordinating with cells and systems, feels like an inner symphony, keeping us balanced and ready for whatever comes next. It's a reminder of how beautifully our bodies are wired to not just survive but thrive.

Sexual acts are the highest physical activity the human body can have which move both in a turbo mode. So, imagine how crucial it is to move your sexual energy for overall health. But when I say sexual, I don't necessarily mean only with sexual acts.

Of course, many other activities move endorphins and molecules. Take exercise, like running in a park or dancing to a favorite song. These activities start a rush of endorphins, our body's natural pain relievers, which travel through the blood to connect with special spots in the brain, easing pain and creating a happy feeling. At the same time, blood carries important stuff like sugar and oxygen to give muscles energy and keep them strong.

Playing sports, like soccer or swimming, does the same. As the heart beats fast, it sends endorphins to lift our mood and reduce aches, while also moving nutrients to help muscles work and heal. Even laughing, like during a fun game or a silly moment with friends, releases endorphins, and blood spreads these and other helpers to clear the mind and boost happiness. Even a simple hug or cuddle helps. These moments spark endorphins to make us feel calm and close to others, while blood moves helpers that lower stress and support our health. From exercise to joyful moments, every activity

creates a flow of these tiny helpers, keeping our bodies strong, full of energy, and ready to shine—a reminder of how amazing our systems are.
energy as a priority because in my 17 years of expertise on this subject, I have proven it's the fastest way for people to release traumas and heal the body from its core, especially if those traumas come from past sexual experiences. Some people think the strongest energy the body creates is with the mind, and that simply is not true. Your mind is what steers the energy your body creates; it's the command center. You do not create life with your thoughts; you create them with your genitals, and if your core is broken, your energy will not flow properly, and your abundance will also be broken.

Sexual energy is what has gotten society to lose its course, so learning to move this energy accordingly will then guide us towards a life or "social energy" which is what humans need to be creating daily for a harmonious world, and believe me, there is nothing sexual about it. But unfortunately, we can't reach social energy without first fixing the twisted generation of sexual energy amongst us.

Our Conduit

Our physical energy channel begins in our mouth and travels through the spinal cord towards the genitalia, distributed through all its surroundings. This is the flow of energy within the human body. It is important to have it as open as possible so that energy can flow freely 24/7. When I mean freely, I mean without you even thinking about it, the spiritual realm will determine when you need to channel energy or not if you are in tune. When you need protection, comfort, reassurance, or healing. If our body is open, it will work on its own without our conscious level commanding it, because it has a mind of its own.

Imagine if you were looking down at Earth and you see all of the humans on it, but you see them as tubes of light, except some of the light bulbs are so dirty they are very dim, and you can't really see them. Then you have ones that are very dark, and the ones that are perfectly lit and clean. We are beams of light connected to the ether.

People who can sing, not necessarily in tune, have their vocal channel side very open; beautiful sounds come from a beautiful connection, not forced, just flowing. Or a person who talks, and you just can't stop listening, and you feel comforted by their voice. Those who are extremely sensitive throughout their body and in love have their sexual energy core and creativity highly active, and their lower channel open. This means someone who feels arousal the same as when they were virgins, always, and by a simple, gentle touch.

When the conduit of the female channel is open, it actually has the ability to open and close as tightly as she wants, from the throat to sing or from the yoni walls to release energy when needed. Elasticity means health at every level. Where there are no traumas, no pain, there are no negative energies, so there should be no illnesses coming from this area.

The male is the antenna that lowers the energy, and the female is the receiver that duplicates the energy and spreads it out, amplifying it. So, it's the female's job to make sure she makes the male feel love so he can always channel positive energy to her and her family. The male will feel what the female makes him feel. As long as there is love and caring involved, anyone can channel positive energy even if not in a relationship. It won't be as strong as channeling with the love of your life, but it will still be positive energy; it's all about intention. How pure are the intentions of this ritual you are about to perform? Are you doing it to please your carnal needs, or are you doing it to channel energy, self-help, help of the other, and progress?

How large your channel depends on how much you have worked on it and in some cases like mine and many others in the world, when you work in expanding your channel and you are born with a mission of energy work, this channel will be a gift of channeling energy for others to heal.

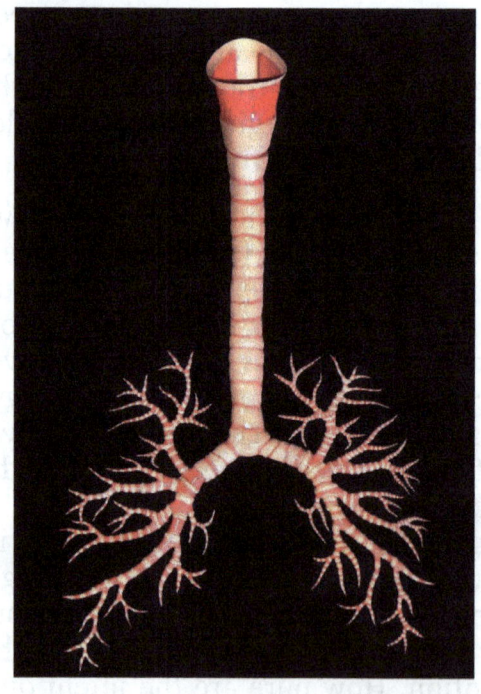

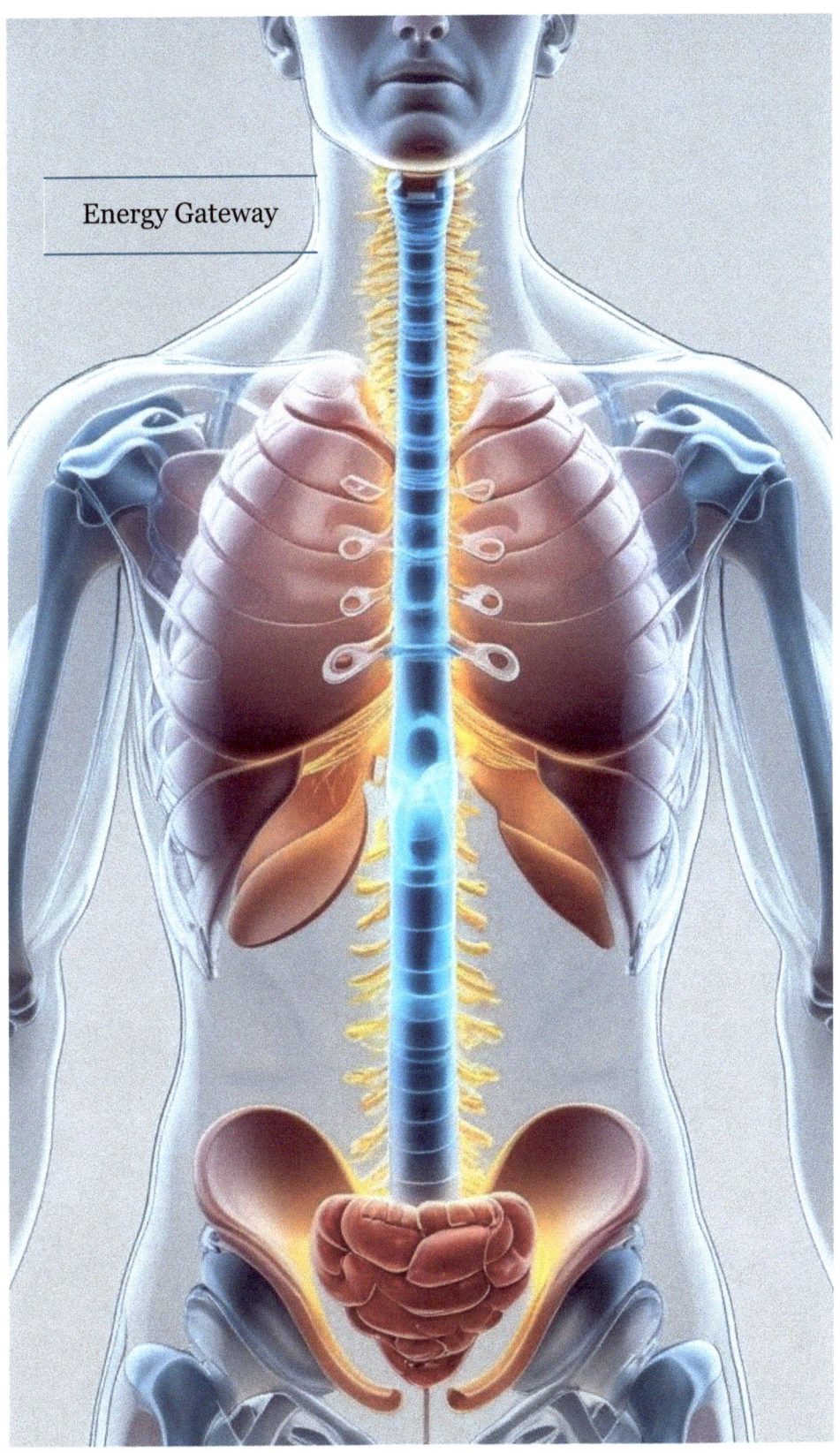
Energy Gateway

The Throat

The throat is something we do not really pay much attention to. It's there, period. Being home to hundreds of sensitive spots, it is the end of our channel where we expel. Our upper body is home to all the overwhelming emotions we decided to hold on to and not release. The words you have never spoken, the feelings you have never shown. Until one day you say, enough of this nonsense, and you start speaking your mind liberating yourself.

Look at the throat in a purely anatomical way, and the vagina the same way; these are exit points, there is truly little difference in structure. The same rings across the way; you can feel some on the top of your mouth with your tongue. The lines you feel on your palate are palatal rugae. These are ridges or folds of mucous membranes on the hard palate, the bony front part of the roof of your mouth. They vary in number and pattern between individuals and can feel like distinct lines or wrinkles when you touch them with your tongue. Rugae help with gripping and manipulating food during chewing and may also play a role in speech and *sensation*.

The beginning of our channel is on our cervix which also consists of having mucous membranes, both for different uses, but both with the goal of sensation.

The tongue, cheeks, and lips all need to be a wave of arousal through the body. If this isn't the case and you don't get aroused only by kissing, then you have dormant sensitive spots and need to activate new ones. Remember your first kiss? Kissing is such a more intimate action than anything else, and it needs to be paid more attention to.

The more arousal and energy that passes through the channel, the more energy will pass along to the throat, expanding the energy through sound. Just like it's true that the eyes are a window to the soul, it's also true that the voice is an essence of our soul when spoken, so our voice must have power.

The Yoni

Your face is as beautiful as your yoni they say. The flexibility of our pelvic rings is very important when it comes to supporting a healthy body. Females have them inside their yoni, and men have them around their lingam. You might not be quite aware of them, but they hold thousands of sensitive spots because these are the propulsors of your engine. These rings need to be stimulated to keep healthy and elastic. Each ring holds several sensitive spots that, when the rings are resting and contracted, are cramped together, but when the rings elongate, these spots line up to one another towards the exterior part of the skin and create octopus-like suctions of energy pulsations. When they are all working properly the instant moment of penetration itself is an orgasmic feeling. If this is not the case, do not worry, everything is reversible with

patience, training, and positive energy; it just takes time.

When a woman has a healthy reproductive system fully functioning with its constant lubrication and feelings of extremely high arousal levels, the action of delivering babies completely changes. You can go from having a traumatic, painful experience to one where you can learn to reach a painless level of elasticity. Remember, just like you can control your throat, you would also be able to control your pelvic walls. There is no better pleasurable act in the world than that of giving life... so why does it have to be painful? I think we are just uneducated about who we really are or what we are capable of doing. Like someone just wiped out our truth, filled it with nonsense information and watched us deteriorate over time while maintaining a sick patient that they can make money from and keep a moving economy. We are meant to live in a world of pleasure, no illnesses, no assisted birth, no pain, no problems. Every time a human intervenes on a body, it's a scar to recover from internally because of the number of sensitive spots harmed at the time of intervention, spots doctors do not see, and science doesn't care to acknowledge.

The more contracted and expanded the yoni is, the more room for pleasure. If at any moment there is discomfort, then you will follow up with exercises.

Find the spot that hurts and work on it by focusing more on the arousal to cover up the pain and release any tension associated with it through an orgasm and release the trauma by replacing it with pleasure consciously. This is something both male and female need to learn, because if you are a man and you fall in love with a wounded woman, it will be your task to help her heal so your relationship flourishes. A whole hand should fit in the yoni, two even, and no pain should exist.

Now there are women that are very stretched but also flaccid. This is due to moments of penetration when the man is too rigid, and the yoni was not lubricated enough, which causes tears to occur anywhere from the entrance to the inside. These are acts of negative energy, so any aggressive action that literally rips the female yoni forcefully open will cause floppiness and loss of sensitivity in the long run, where if this woman doesn't have a man with a very large lingam, she will not feel pleasure and will have lost the ability to tighten and open as needed. These cases are a bit more difficult to heal than if there is too much tightness and pain because it's a reverse exercise, tightening back up the pelvic area.

In either case, with time, if not so already, the yoni walls must feel like clouds. It's the clouds that take you to heaven, the pathway to the soul, as cheesy as that sounds.

When the yoni is healthy, it feels very lubricated, and there is a constant feeling of pleasure. The trick is to start your activity very softly, then softly but deeper, and when you get to the sensitive part, this is where you will bring awareness to your walls and relate the sensitivity you are feeling with where your mind can connect to. Remember, you are exercising your energy vibration. The more you exercise, the faster the yoni will learn to stretch and tighten on its own and slowly release the knots, traumas, or tension you might have. The point you want to get to is embracing that sensitivity so you can feel more pleasure for longer periods of time, and just get your body used to the feeling of the sensitivity so that it becomes more familiar to you and you no longer will feel sensitive but rather always pleasurable.

A yoni that has been accustomed to aggressive behavior will need roughness to feel pleasure; this will unfortunately generate negativity, so if she wants an abundant life, she needs to include tantric teachings into her life, to learn to feel again and open back her sensitivity.

All you need to be is vigilant. Be your own examiner first. Feel your body, every corner of it, study it, and perceive it. Where there is pain, there is blockage. Find it, heal it. It's very simple, but it does take time.

The yoni is the same as your throat; you should be able to open it and close it as needed. When you need it, you are working with muscle memory and tissue memory, so the more you practice your elasticity, the more your body will remember to go there with no struggle. The same with every other part of your body, we are regenerative beings.

The moment the body can do this is in puberty. Just a kiss or the very instance of entrance of penetration should feel like an orgasm; that is the strength of pleasure a woman must have, so imagine orgasming constantly.

Some great exercises to make sure the female Yoni is working properly is working with the hands. The male needs to take responsibility for keeping this area working properly. Gentle massage on the clitoris, which is the bottom where all the yoni nerves and energy spots end up. So, stimulating the clitoris creates a ripple effect that sends electricity towards the yoni walls, allowing you to fully relax every time a little more.

This electricity is obviously felt by the man as waves or currents of pleasure. Therefore, men love to hear and feel the woman feeling pleasure; the energy they release enhances their energy. Once there is a relaxation, the man must now practice in opening the yoni walls with his fingers, from one to eventually the full hand and fist and so on. This, for most people, will take time, and it might even be painful for some, but you must endure it. Everyone is in a different stage when it comes to their sexuality. Never push, always pulse. When there is pain, you must touch the clitoris; this way, it will distract the mind from the pain and focus on the pleasure. The purpose is to unblock these blockages. Every area where there is pain in the yoni, is a part to be worked on to heal. Our pelvic area holds all the tension and trauma of our body, because everything passes through there. Yet society has shamed anything sexual so much that we have forgotten what it feels like to be a woman.

Nodules or knots are something that are created in the walls of the yoni; these are the ones that feel like a rough sensation, where the skin is not as smooth, these are traumas, negativities, stuck emotions. The same tension you can hold onto in your shoulders is something you can carry anywhere else in your body and especially in your pelvic area. If so much attention is paid to the face and back with massages, why would the pelvis and yoni be any different? Our body is all connected, and there is no area that should be unspoken for or unreached. This is why a well-maintained pelvic area means a healthy life. You are released and free of all tension from the root. Let us bring pleasure back to society, where nature and orgasmic birth are a necessity. Let us bring new life into a world of pleasure, not pain.

What you want to do within an exercise, following up, is to find your "rhythm." Depending on where you are at an arousal level. For example, when you begin to feel arousal, make sure you hold on to it, observe it, and whatever you do, do not force an orgasm. On the contrary, think of extending your arousal as much as possible. For this, you will stop your movements when you are on the edge of release. A fully healthy yoni does not need clit manipulation. The clitoris needs to be seen as a button on the cover of a pressure cooker, when there is too much energy being stored in your vulva, it will create sensitivity and pressure to release, so by pressing or gently massaging the clit, you are releasing the extra pressure that your body can't bear to hold. The truth is that the more open you are, the more energy you will be able to hold or store without the feeling of sensitivity and needing to release. In fact, the sensitivity becomes a constant pleasure, and you will no longer feel the need to touch the clit so often.

Do not become clit dependent. This is the worst thing you could do because you are crippling your body by adjusting it to only feel pleasure when touching the clit. Women who usually do this do so because of the discomfort or pain, so they replace that feeling with the clitoris sensation. But if this becomes a new way of pleasure altogether, it will leave out the importance of the pleasure you should be feeling just by penetration. Use the clitoris as a magic button, where you only use it when needed to release tension, pain or sensitivity, and use it to impulse your arousal but with control. For example, if you are in a healthy condition, you will want to use the clitoris gently, and when you feel you are reaching a new sensitivity you can't handle, that's where you would use it, without reaching a forced orgasm.

When you adapt yourself to stop right before you release, and if you really pay attention, you will feel a wave that will go from your coccyx through your yoni and out. This wave of heat and energy is what will lubricate and expand your yoni to be penetrated deeper, so you now reach a new frequency altogether, and now the pleasure should feel different.

Each relaxation of your pelvis is a next step into a new wave of energy. When you force an orgasm, you are limiting the potential growth of your energy's expansion, because by teaching it that that is the max you can handle before it explodes you are restraining it from its level of expansion.

When you learn not to release that wave of energy, you train your body to exhale it through your full channel from your genitals to your mouth. An open mouth and deep exhales should be natural at this stage and if not, try to implement it anyway to help you get there. Sound is the bass of energy, so whatever sound you release through this activity is an augmentation of the energy being released to the ether.

The Yoni has a mind of its own, and if you are a man, you need to learn to listen to it, feel it, sense it, connect, and communicate with it. Men should never force themselves in where they are not invited, so even if you are in a situation of intimacy, when the yoni is not ready, it simply is not ready, and you need to prepare it for dilation. Pay attention to how the blood starts to flow, and the clit starts to get fuller as arousal happens. When you are ready to have any kind of penetration, being hand or lingam, pay attention to how the yoni feels and tease it. Teasing will always allow for the expansion of it faster.

When you try any elasticity exercises with the hands as a couple, this is when you will learn to feel the yoni and its reactions even more, which is a perfect way to get to know your partner and their limits and see the progress as you go. You will notice that the yoni will request more by tightening and closing, which usually means it needs more friction and deeper. If you feel you are pushing at any moment, you are forcing the situation, and what we are looking for is for the hands to be sucked in rather than forcing themselves in. Pay attention to the body's movements and reactions to know what feels good and do not be afraid to ask; communication is key.

Society has completely reversed the use of what sex should be by making us numb, with quickies, and shallow, making it all about reaching the orgasm. When the truth is, it's never been about the orgasm because we are supposed to live in a constant level of orgasm, not just feel it for seconds at a time. We are meant to live connected to a constant pleasure of living, and most of the world is connected to carnal sex, fear, shame, and hate.

Elasticity is something we lose, so working on this from when puberty ends and beyond is deeply necessary to maintain a healthy body, and as an adult, anywhere, from once a month it would be recommended to maintain its elasticity intact. If you are someone who needs to recover from a lot of pain or rigidity, it will take time. Each day, you will work a little more, allow yourself to rest in between, and continue. Consistency is key. Just as if you were training at the gym, here you are training your internal yoni walls and overall health. Once you reach a full elastic yoni, you will not only live in constant pleasure, but you will also notice an incredible number of changes in your life. How long? It all depends on how much trauma you have held on to.

Can you tell which one is the throat and which one is the yoni?

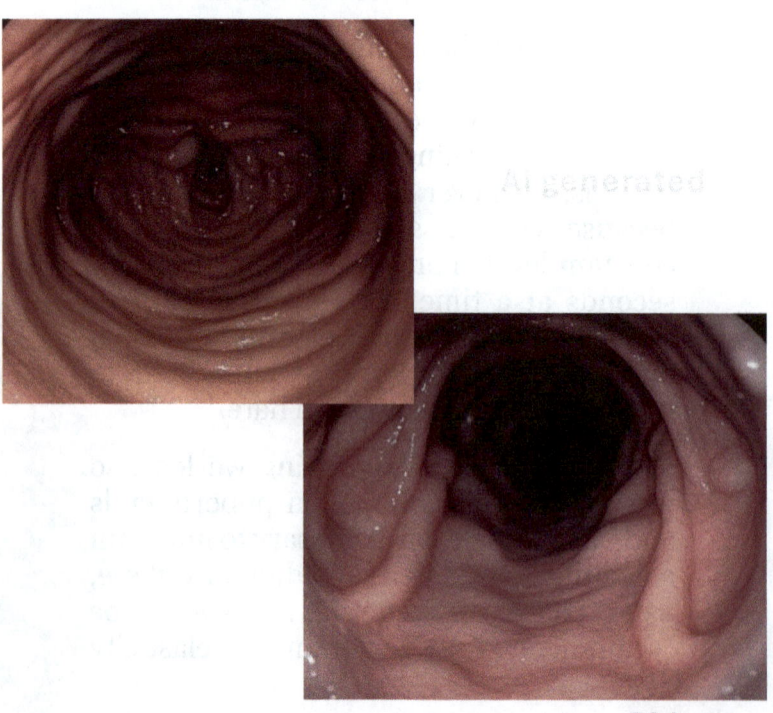

EXERCISE FOR FEMALE STRETCH

I recommend you stretch your body before you begin. Yoga basic stretches for your glutes, pelvis, legs, back, and neck. Find your favorites. 5, 10 min stretch.

The best exercise to heal the female and reset her sexual pleasure state is the stretching of the rings, yoni walls, with toys, cucumbers, or even better, a partner's hands. The hands are a perfect tool because they can spread; you should be practicing this as often as possible, daily if you can, if you want to see results and fast. The time at which you will know you are done and only need maintenance is when everything feels pleasurable. No pain, no discomfort.

The male partner will be using both hands in a backwards praying position. Starting with a soft stimulation of the clitoris first, to help relax the area massage the chest, back to the clit, the idea is to activate the whole body. Get lots of natural oil. I like mixing coconut and castor oil. Do not use chemicals; use nature. The male needs to learn to perceive the female; the body will talk to you, expressing what it's ready for. Once you feel the clit is filling up a little bit and feel a little arousal, you will go in with one finger, moving consistently but gently. The yoni will let you know when it's dilated enough to take more in; think of it as a living being. The yoni will contract and tighten as well as loosen. When you feel it's tight but with a little more room, is when it's time to go in with another finger. Connection is everything; you need to really connect with what it is requesting. This is something that should be done slowly and always keeping in mind to have arousal present. Arousal is the same as dilation.

The more fingers that go in, the more aroused you should be, but nothing should be done with forcing, only slow pulsations until it invites you in. If you must push, you are forcing it. If there is discomfort, this is when you work on the discomfort to release the trauma and continue another day. Never go further if you can't release the pain, which will be your task for that exercise, to release that trauma, and so on. With this exercise, you will focus on opening the channel by stretching. It is very important to breathe deeply and consciously. Try to relax the joints and muscles of your pelvic area; the more relaxed, the more open the hips and pelvis will be.

What are you feeling? I need you to be aware of things like: do you feel any pain anywhere? Does it feel like it's pinching somewhere? Is it dry or irritated? Start making a list of all your emotions the first time, so you can bring awareness to them. Normally, if you have any kind of discomfort, you will feel very irritated by the discomfort; it can be so strong that it can take away any pleasure. Instead of putting focus on what feels good, you are immediately pushed towards the pain or being uncomfortable. It is important to be patient on both sides. Trauma is not released in one session, and this will of course obviously be more effective if it's done with a person who cares for you, so energy influences the healing. However, if you decide to proceed, you must do it with the intention of healing, both the facilitator and the receiver. The facilitator must understand that he is doing a service and exercise.

Because pain is trauma, it's also negative energy. Negativity will always have a resistance to your healing, frustrating you, making you feel worse, but since we already know this and we are intelligent beings, our intelligence will surpass any current blockages. If you already know that, when you are having a discomfort at the time of generating sexual energy, that discomfort is a negative blockage, so go against its will of pain and control the pain until it is no longer there, replace pain with pleasure with pure thoughts. You decide what is part of your body; pain and fear should not be part of your body. Also, keep in mind that not every day is the same, nor is your body at the same disposal.

If you want higher pleasure, higher orgasms, the female genitalia have to heal and work as nature intended them to.

The yoni massages are strong and sometimes painful, but if you persevere, you will reach pleasure levels of which you have never dreamed.

You will go from pleasure to pain, to discomfort, burning, numbness, healing, resting, recovering, and more pleasure again.

"The more elastic the conduit is, the better the energy performance; when it opens, it is like a flower blooming and releasing its colors, calling to the bees" – Meditators-

Female Progress (Express everything you are feeling and how its releasing)

Week one

Week two

Week three

Week four

Pain is something people get used to feeling so much that they get to the point of forgetting what pleasure ever meant. You are not meant to feel pain or fear; you are meant to live in pleasure.

Practice your exercise and see how far you can go. Remember, the more elastic the better the channel. Having control of our elasticity is controlling our creative energy. We can close the faucet or open it whenever you want. Each time you practice this, you should feel better elasticity, no more discomfort, more focused, and once it's healed, your maintenance will be light and pleasurable.

Making the yoni elastic and strengthening the muscles so that it opens and closes easily with fluidness and without pain, this action will keep the yoni canal and uterus free of polyps. So, these exercises will keep you off the hospital bed and off the doctor's meds if treated responsibly and consistently.

The yoni canal must be maintained; if it is not in use, it's closed, it's like a cloth hose, it flattens together, the walls touch and create contamination, maintaining particles that end up germinating into viruses or infections.

Another thing that needs to be addressed is the progress of your fluids. It's normal to have discharge as your body is constantly cleansing itself, plus it's your energy fluid. Try to give up any toxic products, any products that are not natural and have scents or chemicals that you're absorbing directly in one of the most sensitive areas of your body, affecting your hormones directly. Anything that affects lymphatic locations, like your deodorant, body lotions, tampons, pads, get rid of anything that has chemicals from penetrating your skin. If you are suffering from something like dryness, I would highly recommend using a cucumber with small cuts and bathing it with castor oil. According to my personal testimony on this, we have proven that the juices on the cucumber are extremely beneficial for the hydration of the yoni walls.

When the body is not producing fluids, which is the same as energy in some cases, it's a sign that something is not working properly. Starting with the physical part, which is straight to the exercises, will eventually with time, also start to balance this as well.

The Lingam

The male lingam (penis) is the antenna to the energy, and the male has absolutely no control over it; he can only have control of his thoughts, and it will erect according to the energy that is filling it. Genitals are 100% powered by energy. Every lingam is a key to a different frequency and existence. The symbol of the lingam used to be seen as a good luck symbol, as it is the representation of fertility and life. With society switching its knowledge and information to being hidden, now it's seen as perversion, the total opposite of what it really means, because people started channeling negative energy instead of positive. Strip clubs and brothels are common, yet sexual health or tantric spaces are rare and limited.

The lingam has many energetic identifications when it comes to erections, so you can identify if you are channeling positive energy or negative energy. For starters, understand that in an encounter, the female is the one that incentivizes the male to which energy he will be connecting to, unless he already has an intention with the woman of sleeping with her alone, then it will be negative by nature. If the woman is connecting to negativity, then she will make the male channel negativity; if she's loving and caring, she will make the man connect to positivity. Therefore, women today are attacked by negative energy to disrupt the male from channeling positive energy. Women today have become overtly sexual.

The lingam is supposed to be caressed slowly, gently, with love, passion, and softness so that throughout the practice of the massage, it can start to channel positive energy for the woman to receive. Just like in life, easy things come with negativity, and positivity will take more work; it's the same here. Negative energy will always be around trying to have you connect to it, so before moving on to the physical urge, you must relax, calm down, go on, and focus on channeling positive energy, which is a more connected feeling of arousal and a heightened nonphysical state. If you are in a loving relationship, moments of passion do not need to be controlled; you will undeniably be creating positive energy without aggression. Do not confuse passion with aggression. One is filled with love; the other is filled with lust and is cathartic.

Every ring on the male lingam is, as for a woman, a ring of sensitive spots and electric currents. So, the more aware the male is of his lingam's sensitivity, the more pleasure he will feel. The lingam can also suffer from sensitivity loss if used in very aggressive methods for a long period of time. The male lingam is not supposed to be stretched over its normal limit as it's forcing the sensitive spots to be in an extreme stretching position, which is only supposed to happen when the male is about to release to the woman, or in moments of pulsation, of engorgement and release. These moments nature made for them only to be had when both female and male are wanting to conceive.

When a man has an instant, very rigid erection towards someone, it's because he is channeling negative energy. The position of the lingam in an erection and the energy it is connected to goes as follows:

1. The lingam positioned DOWN is incredibly positive.
2. The lingam positioned STRAIGHT is positive.
3. The lingam positioned UP RIGHT is negative.
4. The lingam positioned UP LEFT is negative.
5. The lingam positioned UP straight is overly aggressive and very negative.

These are physical views of how energy presents itself in a male.

So basically, up to either side is negative, down or straight either way is positive.

If the male has suffered from an aggressive youth and somehow hurt the lingam with these actions, in some cases, they will endure with what is known as Peyronie's disease, which is trauma to the lingam. In this case, it is difficult to know if they are channeling negative or positive energy, but it's a shown factor that they were aggressive at some point, so it's important to train the man to not become rigid and learn to feel through softness and love again. The position will remain, but the energy will change.

If you are a man and are thinking, "mine goes up and I'm not thinking aggressively." You do not have to think or act aggressively because, remember, you channel involuntarily and have no control over it. What you need to figure out is when you became a negative energy channel. If you were very promiscuous in puberty, this is the training you gave to your body. Promiscuity does not work unless you think of venting and aggressive acts because there is no feeling involved with someone you do not love, so your body picked up this channel, and later in life, you will continue to channel this energy because your body inherited it as a habit. So, mental training in tantric habits needs to come in and retrain your brain to command your channel back to positivity, with time, you will notice the difference. But just like with women, you will feed those urges to be aggressive or unfaithful or have chemistry changes as well. Learning how to effectively use the lingam with gentleness will be a journey. Mental strength is necessary. You may also just find a woman who has a shield, and you will create a perfect match, because you both need aggression, but with time, tantric practices are highly recommended if you want to attract abundance in life.

If men only know love, they will only channel love; it is up to the woman to provide this comfort and connection.

Soft vs Hard

In this chapter, I will copy and paste an email directly from Dr. Pedro Joaquín Valencia.

"Working to generate energy in couples is an act of love, but for those who lack love and do so by mutual agreement in pursuit of positive energy, it is done very slowly, with a rhythm that seeks pleasure rather than yoni destruction from emotional release. It is a delicate process that keeps the woman in continuous pleasure. (tantra)

They might work at it for a long time, not just a few minutes, stretching out the pleasure. The woman begins to crave more rhythm, speed, or gentle intensity without harm, regulating it herself rather than the man, and she may ask for it to be faster.

Positive energy is generated through love because someone with love would never treat their partner aggressively. Couples who do not seek that love, or even know about energy or positivity, are the ones who start intimacy sooner than expected. is that a woman begins to feel pleasure when she "plays" with the male lingam, touching it repeatedly and treating it like a toy that brings her joy. because the male lingam is an antenna for energy, which can be positive or negative, depending on the situation. The more it is touched and rubbed, the more energy is created. But two very distinct things happen. A woman who had a sexually active adolescence needs that lingam to be hard—the harder, the better. A woman who did not have sexual experience in adolescence and is in a relationship for the first or only time, prefers to play with a soft member, sometimes very soft and small—the smaller, the better. with an extremely high active sexual adolescence says: "I don't like a soft member; I prefer it hard, otherwise it lacks masculine strength." without a sexual adolescence says: "It's awful when it gets hard; I like it soft, gentle, and to caress it." (This comes from our study of thousands of female patients we have evaluated for our conferences.)

The same applies to penetration. A woman without a sexual adolescence will never enjoy a partner with an extremely hard lingam. We also know well that hardness causes damage and, over time, leads to yoni health issues. In contrast, loving couples who always approach it gently and with a semi-soft lingam never face yoni health consequences. must be careful because a very rigid lingam can harm the yoni making it produce defensive acids (chemical fluids), and those acids sometimes attack the lingam, causing injuries or small cuts, this is not a disease, but it is an uncomfortable burning sensation that happens out of self-defense."

- Dr. Pedro Joaquín Valencia, Spain.

Excessive rigidity channels more negativity. Soft and tender is positive; this is because it will make the female feel warmth and not friction. When I say soft, I do not mean it shouldn't be erect; there is a semi-rigid form which is perfect, but this is something that should be lifted by the female incentive.

As we have learned throughout the chapters, I will remind you that if you are someone who has gotten used to aggressive sex throughout puberty, unfortunately, this will be something you will always need. Your body needs a taste of its own medicine. So, when you fall in love and your partner wants to treat you with kindness and softness you must train yourself to feel gently again, but you will always need that aggression every now and then to stabilize your body's needs. Lots of health issues are related to this incredibly unique physical need for your body to find its balance again.

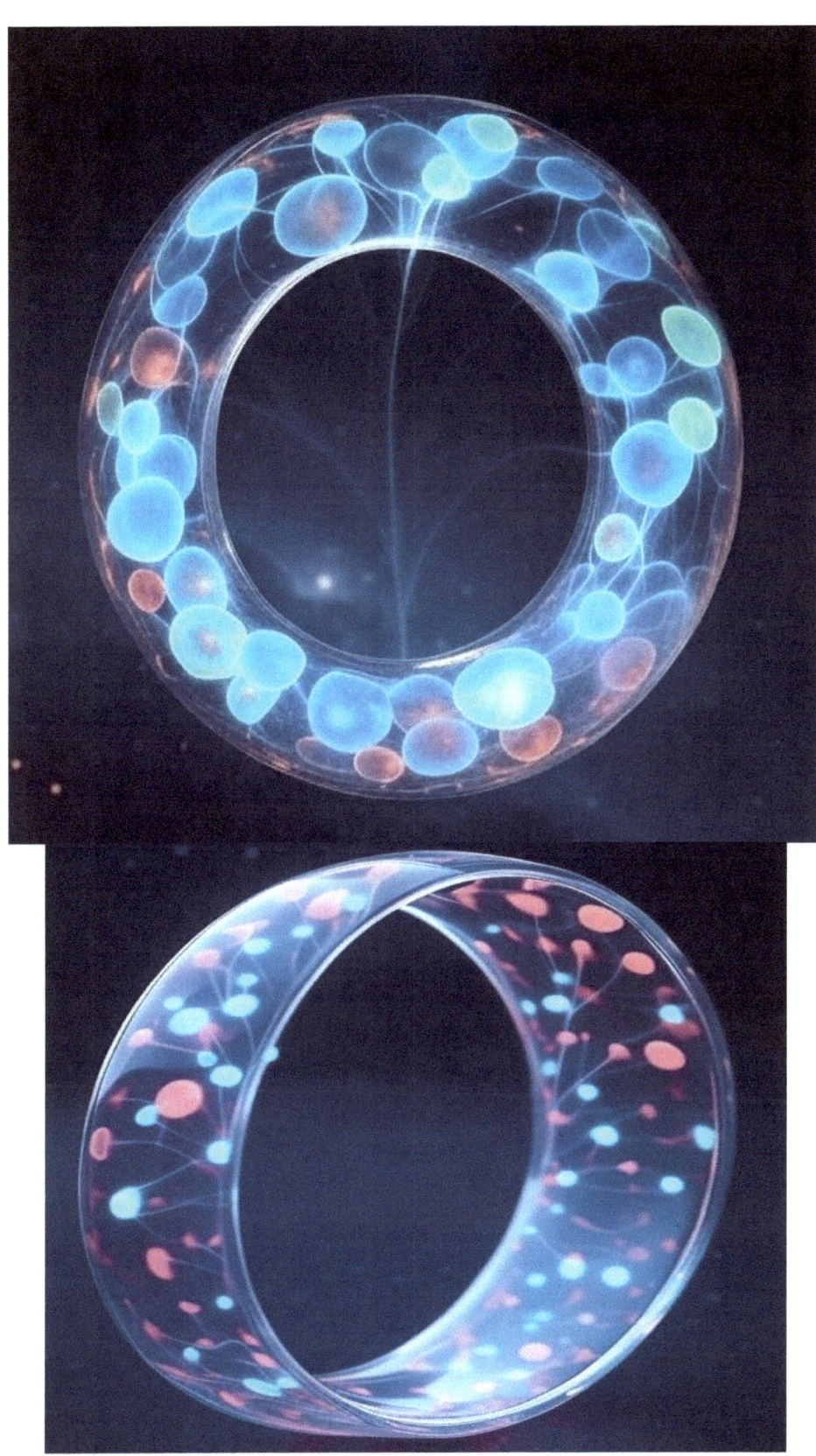

Orgasm

The energy that fills you, that you accumulate. The strength to your channel and your abundance is how much energy you are storing, and when do you need to release it because you are overflowing with energy. If that energy is purely concentrated in your root chakra, you will feel an uncomfortable urge to release. Imagine, now knowing that this is your fuel, why would you forcefully release it when it is not necessary? It will just keep you running on empty. In a perfect body and a perfect natural world, an orgasm should always come naturally and never be forced.

If we dig deeply into creation, an orgasm's purpose is to bring life into this world, or when the male has arousal, meaning he is channeling energy that needs to be given to the woman, because he is the antenna. Men have erections without thinking about it, and it is because they are solely manipulated by energy. If they are connected to positive energy, their erection will be steady but not rough or very rigid. If their erection is negative, they will be extremely rigid and usually point upwards. In the case of a man being in a loving relationship and having spontaneous erections, this is a sign of a higher energy letting him know he needs to charge his partner; in this case, it should be received orally. The male channels energy, and the female charges up her body with energy to then amplify; it is a perfect symbiosis. Anything you do really generates energy, but doing it this way, you will benefit more from energy.

In single cases, it would happen with self-cleansing, which is the way to remove contaminated energy from the body, which normally would not happen if you were in a loving relationship because you maintain yourself. Our body's exhaust is also done through orgasms, meaning any toxic energy you might be absorbing from the surrounding environments will need to be released through an orgasm. In this case, it is important to check its consistency, if your release is thick and white, it's toxic energy, which is great. If your release is runny or transparent, it's positive energy, even better (it has nothing to do with testosterone levels), we are speaking energy. To be sure, you can get a testosterone check and then, once you know, start analyzing your cleansing. Cleansing of one's body is not just masturbation; it's a conscious release of toxic energy, meaning you will not cleanse just by masturbating; you need to do it consciously and absorb positive energy from a source or partner to push out the toxic energy. Our body is a space. When positive energy fills it, it will push out any negative energy, but if you leave an empty space, it will need to be filled quickly.

Orgasms should come naturally, with no forced friction or speedy process; this should not be the goal. Different from what you have heard of or are used to doing. Nature's way is for our bodies to have orgasms all throughout the day. Just like what happened when you were going through puberty. This wetness is constant energy surges and the body's way of auto-cleansing itself. When your body releases the stored energy, it's like you used up all the energy bottled up, and you need to start over filling up your tank again. When you do not release, you will just continue to charge with energy, use the amount your body needs, and maintain yourself in an active, natural, open state where energy flows continuously and your channel stays open. This is when everything in life flows.

People go out of their way to reach orgasms because in most of the world's civilizations, it's misunderstood. If you live in a constant orgasmic pleasurable state, you will not have the physical need or desire to release or even feel carnal pleasure. If you don't live it, you can't possibly understand it. There are certain cultures that understand the importance of energy, but unfortunately, instead of teaching it, some have created strict rules or prohibitions to try to prevent people from generating negative energy. I believe people should have free will over their bodies, but also the right information to choose what seems right for them. It is a part of our journey to learn and grow.

When a woman loses sensitive spots (energy connections), she will begin to close her channel quite fast, normally leading to a clit dependency, meaning you can't feel aroused unless you touch the clit, which basically means you are upside down in how you're supposed to be. All the labia and within has sensitive spots, if you have gotten used to releasing only with a specific motion or touch, you have made your body dependent on that action, when really you should be focusing on feeling more with less.

The more you train your body and mind to relax and regain control, the more sensitive you will become to touch. Depending on how disconnected you are to your sensitivity is how long it will take you to regain feeling. If you think back to when you were a teen and were going through puberty, you could have the feeling of an orgasm just by kissing someone. This is what an open channel feels like and how orgasmic you should feel throughout the day. That was your body fully functional.

When you touch the clitoral region, it produces arousal accompanied by increasingly intense pleasure. The yoni has the ability to generate pleasure 10 to 12 times greater than the clit, which means it is pointless to seek arousal and pleasure in the clitoris when the yoni generates much greater pleasure. This is because the yoni walls, along their length and circumference, have thirty times more sensitive points than the clitoral region, but the most important thing is that inside there is the so-called 'G-spot'. leave the dependency of the clit, but not impossible, because for the most part, you will do this as a necessity to release pain or tension normally due to the lack of natural lubrication, but this will eventually also lead you to become more crippled in your sexuality.

The clitoris is where all the sensitive points meet, so paying more attention to it will cause the woman to stop focusing on the important area which is the pleasurable feeling of the yoni walls. If lubrication happens naturally, there will always be pleasure. What causes discomfort for women is the lack of natural lubrication, creating a sense of scraping rather than sliding.

What is an orgasm to you?

Energetically, an orgasm is the feeling of connection you have to the ether. You call it an orgasm because you've made it a casual every now and then feeling because you forgot that you once lived in an orgasmic state, full of energy in your younger years, fully connected. An orgasm is the release of excess energy from our body; it is the only way our body knows how to express its connection to our source, via a scream, a moan, or a shiver. How strong is your channel and how much can you channel?

What happens to the body as we age is stiffness and rigidness, because of a lack of physical activity and more desk hours. The more you disconnect, the harder it will be to reach arousal or an orgasmic state. We need to find a balance between self and material.

Imagine your body in a moment of arousal, where what you are doing is elevating your soul to reach the ether. If you are connected to the ether, you will reach a full body orgasm in the first 15 seconds because penetration alone will be orgasmic. This is when the feeling of love is so strong that you both rapidly connect on an ethereal level. It's not just physical. It is easier for men to be connected as men aren't exposed as the female is. The female is the one to mainly suffer ruptures, creating trauma in the pelvic area, affecting the whole body's function. This is why it's also important for men to learn this, so the treatment from male to female becomes gentler. Men have been known to confuse manly with dominant, and in nature, we are meant to work together.

Most women misunderstand when the man who loves them releases too quickly, and they judge the act of pre-ejaculation. The reality is that in most cases, the man is so deeply involved emotionally with the woman that the feeling is too much to control, and they can't help it. They have been accumulating this desire and love, and the feeling overpowers them. Whereas if the woman wasn't that important to him, he would probably be able to move relentlessly until it physically explodes. Therefore, the use of the hands is also so important. Stop making your genitals be the center of everything and change it towards the handwork.

Early release normally will happen when it is the first time you share an intimate act with the person you chose. The following acts will be of longer lasting, and this should also be where the male learns to move this energy through the body with breath, without having it accumulate all in one area, making it unbearable. The accumulation of too much energy in the pelvic area will respond to your release, whereas with breath work you would be moving the energy through your body.

In a perfect world, with two perfect working physical bodies, the normal average time for a couple to last before an orgasm when having intercourse is anywhere from 1 to 3 minutes, sometimes seconds, on their first encounter. From there on, they can slowly begin to enhance their channel to move energy for longer periods of time and more amounts of energy. It's energy flow, which is what you are doing; you are flowing energy up and down and around.

A crucial factor in reaching higher connections is relaxation. If our body is tense, our energy will not flow so swiftly. For the energy to flow more smoothly, there needs to be a feeling of surrender. Surrender to how your body wants to move and not have to think about controlling how it's moving. Most men follow what they learned in porn, and that is far from what should be done.

The next key to having a powerful orgasm is to not rush it. The more you accumulate energy throughout the days or weeks, the more pleasurable the encounter will be because the energy will be higher. Learning to move the energy, if possible, by focusing and acknowledging what you are feeling below. Relaxing the sensation with deep, slow breaths through the nose and throughout the practice, an open mouth, which will help you exhale any excess energy until you reach the moment of orgasm, where your mouth allows any natural noise to exhale from your channels end. This voice acts like a bass system to our energy; it pulses it and pushes it out filling up any corners and reaching wider lengths with your energy. If you want to try heightened states of DMT produced by your own energy, you can try using breath work within the practice.

The issue here is relationships that do not face the fact that the woman has a loss of sensitive spots or a shield. So, months into the relationship, the female arousal starts to disappear, especially after 27 and more increasingly after 35. So, it's very important for women who suffer from shields or loss of sensitive spots to work with their hands and mouth to be able to balance out the time their partner puts into creating arousal in them. If the woman doesn't do anything to heal her shield or awaken new sensitive spots, she will more than likely be headed for a future loneliness. Men eventually get tired of having to work at the arousal that never comes, and the woman misinterprets that her man doesn't arouse her. Sex must not become a job; it should be a passionate, pleasurable act done with all desire.

Generating positive sexual energy for extended periods of time has an amazing reaction in our lives and in the universe; it fills the ether with positivity. By changing the ways in which we use this energy, we can change a lot of outcomes in our life and the planet. The problem today is people are filling the ether with negativity, affecting everyone.

The highest orgasm you can train your body to have is the one when your air is missing. At the moment of the orgasm, not before, the male has to cut the air directly on the throat area, slowly applying pressure and of course listening to the partner's demands. Cutting the air flow at that precise time will be an exercise to hold the explosion of energy within the body and not let it leave, this is to be taken slowly and with the advance of this it will allow the person to connect to the energy source, sometimes even seeing a white light. The more you cut the air, the higher the energy that is stored inside the body. Gently and with time, the connection will be higher; do not produce harm.

The mount of Venus on a woman is where they store their energy, just like men do in their testicles. Some women are chosen to be stores of energy, just like some men are chosen to be higher channels of energy.

Man, sometimes, is used to feeling pleasure out of having control and dominance, and it needs to be a joint task, where the woman seduces the man to activate, and the man channels the energy, which should be drunk or delivered on top of the body. If you are with your partner, they will benefit from this cream.

Think of every level of arousal as being one level of frequency, where it moves your molecules, producing electric shocks. Then, you connect so deeply that you no longer feel your body, you feel current running through your body, and you have a tantric orgasm in a continuous loop. These energetic orgasms are the same feeling as a regular orgasm. The huge difference is that you will only release in a continuous, very long flow instead of the normal orgasm, which is a very fast, highly extreme sensation, and it goes away. In an energetic orgasm, you may be constantly releasing runny fluids, experience a long state of elevation and intensity of pleasure, which is energy widely passing through the body. This is pure energy, and it's usually transparent. This happens instead of you releasing little bits of lubrication and then dense energy all at once, which your body has condensed and needs to dispose of. In an energetic orgasm, your body is secondary but is working side by side with your consciousness or intention to connect and generate positive energy. So, you may reach levels of high astral projection, sacred geometry, visions, and travel where time doesn't exist. You can have multi orgasmic feelings with no movement at all. When you reach this level, you never see sex the same again.

If we heal our bodies and learn to live in a pleasurable state, we will no longer feel the need to feed any lust because we simply won't feel the need.

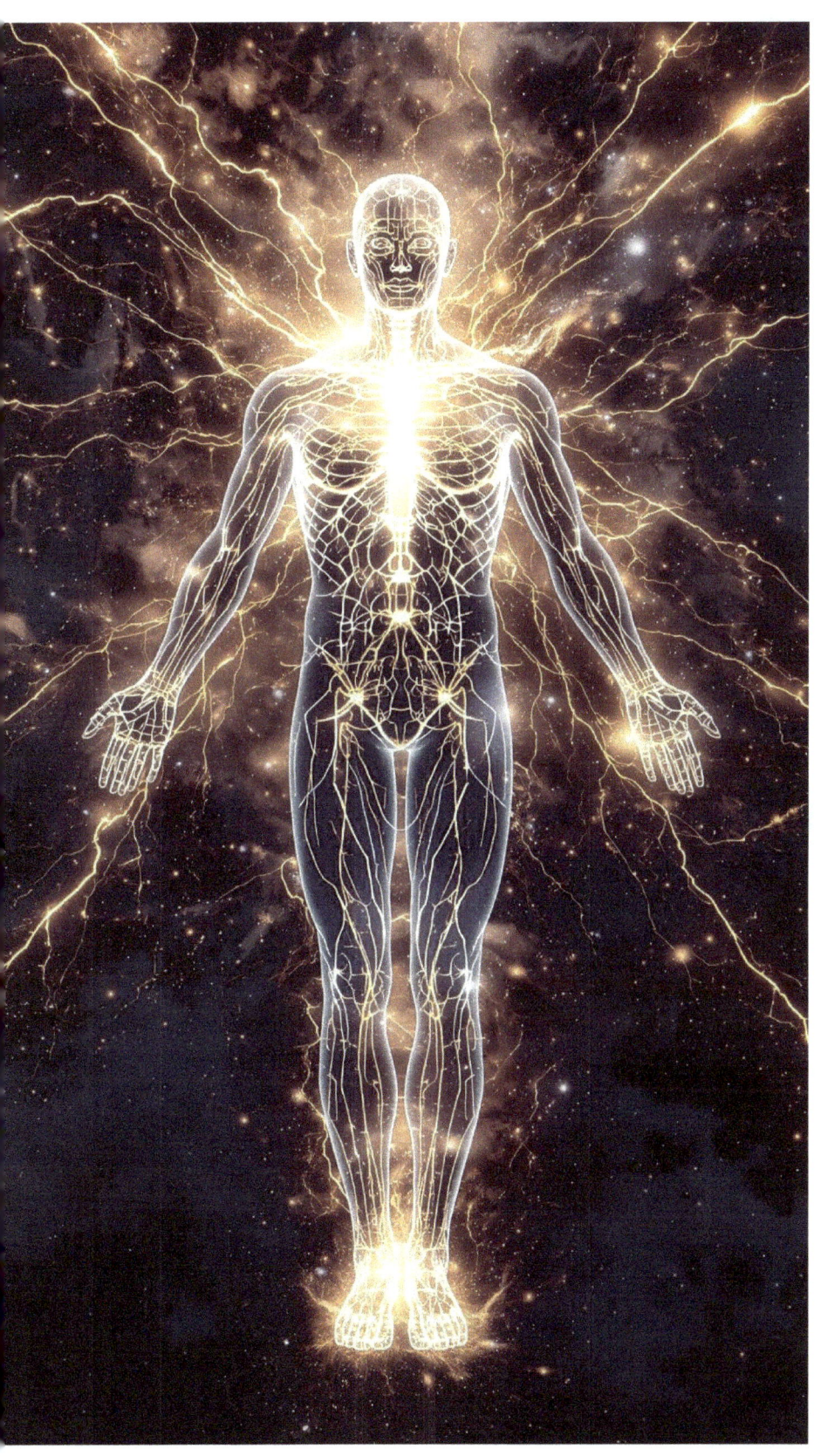

Pleasure:
What Level Are You In?

On a scale of 1 to 10, 10 being the highest, which level would describe your pleasure level?

For most people, their pleasure will always be perceived as at the highest level, because that is all they have been exposed to recently, and they have forgotten that there is much more. The level of your orgasm will determine how high your soul reaches and how connected you are. If you can connect fast or are always connected, you will have amazingly fast arousal or throughout the whole day. If you take time to get aroused, it's because you are very disconnected, but don't panic.

When a man touches a woman's breast he will get an erection in seconds; when a woman touches a man's genitals, she should react the same. If there is a slow reaction for arousal to occur, that means the body has a chemical imbalance. Your energy is out of tune. You should be able to get aroused only by thinking about it. The natural reaction for a body when it is aroused is wetness. This is our body in perfectly functioning condition.

Each physical and emotional trauma will eventually take a toll on your sexual energy parts. The physical trauma that you might not see but goes around internally happens every time you have ever had pain. When something is done forcefully and not naturally or with gentleness, you risk having tears, internal or external, sometimes. But the internal one is the one that damages sensitive spots. These are the ones no one talks about and matter the most. One thing is acting upon the act of generating energy with patience and time, and another is fast or forceful situations.

You will know if your channel is open fully when you have a clear mind, self-love, confidence, and constant natural lubrication throughout the day.

Below will be a list of pleasure measurements to see where you are, from one being crucial to 10, how you should be:

1. You don't have sexual desire.
2. You don't have penetration because of pain.
3. You are numb.
4. You are always dry.
5. You have some intimacy, but with a lot of pain.
6. You have some intimacy, but with discomfort.
7. You take too long to get aroused.
8. You have some intimacy with pleasure.
9. You have lots of intimacy with intense pleasure.
10. You are always aroused, wet, active, and creative.

Level 10 is reaching what we would know as the God tune. This means you are always in a heightened state where life feels like a constant, fulfilled pleasure of existence. This is the alpha stage where your body is constantly channeling, and you are constantly manifesting.

It is the man's job to maintain and pleasure the woman according to her needs to feel pleasure; if the woman doesn't feel pleasure, the man doesn't feel pleasure. The woman's job is to make sure the man feels love and can channel just that, love, but she must put effort into healing if any sensitive spots have been lost in order to have a normal arousal level. What you make the other person feel is what you will receive back.

The more focus each person has on each other's progress in growth, the more both will progress in life.

If you are in a relationship with a woman who has the consequences of a shield, you will just need a little more communication and patience to get from point 1 to 10. It's possible.

Everything is in your head. Your body and soul can find the right person, but if your shield and mind are distracted, you will not see it. So, begin by being aware of what you are feeling and why.

Desire

Desire is always related to engaging in intimacy, but it should not be like that; intimate actions are the result of a consequence that should not always be used sexually. The meaning of intimacy has been lost because pleasure in adolescents leads them to engage in intimacy, and people don't understand that this intimacy was created by nature SOLELY for conceiving children and to make conceiving them pleasurable. But no one understands it this way, except in some places in the Middle East, where natural feelings still endure.

For this reason, there is the use of fingers and the use of the mouth, which are rejected by many due to a lack of cultural understanding from adolescence. Desire is a natural sensation that leads to actions that people have changed, NOT for progress, but for promiscuity.

There is an increasing supply of promiscuous sites that the weak cannot resist, and at the same time, it is a matter of status in high executive circles. Couples do not have to engage in penetration with their lingam; instead, they should work with fingers and the mouth, and only when they are certain they can form a family should they have relations during fertile moments. But nothing is like that.

There is also the need to generate positive energy when there is a need for male masturbation or the oral stimulation provided by the woman, and in those cases, that liquid should be spread over the body and even sometimes consumed because the intention of that act is to transform you into a positive state.
- 27 Meditators –

Desire has been replaced by lust, and the act of intimacy has been lost; the act of sex alone has taken over most. Desire means accumulating this energy for overall progress in life, where there is a constant flame awake in a relationship, and that consistent energy flow is what makes everything around you work flawlessly.

It is altering to recommend you stop having penetration because we live in a society that has already gotten used to this use of their sexual energy. But what you can do is space out these acts a little more, only in moments of need, and try to use our hands and mouth more to see if you feel any difference in your body and overall life. Try this for some weeks and evaluate if it's something that works for you. If it doesn't, then continue as always.

The importance of desire is that it needs to be generated constantly. The desire for your partner on every level is what will have your molecules and endorphins moving, keeping you healthy. So be active in teasing, playing, touching, hugging, and kissing as much as you want to spark that flame, and the longer you can keep that flame going without releasing, the more benefits you will see around you. This is because your body's engine is working fully, and its energy is flowing constantly.

Do not rush to get things over with because you don't have time. You put priorities on things that have nothing to do with your health or well-being, so when it comes to paying attention to your life's flame, do not track time. The more you tease, the more energy that will emerge from each other's bodies like a ticking bomb. Remember, it is not about reaching the end; it's about enjoying the pleasure that accumulates with time. The more time and the more you can hold it throughout the days, the more you will feel alive. You will feel a sense of playfulness that will make you smile throughout the day.

For some couples who have lost their flame and need to get it back, physical exercise like the ones in the other chapters are a must. But there are also some things you can do to spark up the relationship that have nothing to do with sexual acts. Little things like dressing up for your partner, looking nice, and taking care of yourself. Role play where you can create a fantasy together by acting as different people. Reenact the day you met where you met. Going out and keeping the youth alive, why is it that couples in their younger years love to go out, and later in their relationship, they stop taking care of themselves and stop having fun?

You are only as alive as you allow yourself to be, and age should not be dimming down your youth. Desire goes so much further; it is a desire and fire of living, of laughing, of loving, of caring, and of existing. That is the fire that will ignite your relationship. Doing things out of your comfort zone, compromising your dislikes to please your partner, being selfless, and not demanding everything be the way you want it to be.

The moment you lose a sense of who you used to be is the moment you will lose your desire because your happiness will dim. You should never become someone else to please another. You should always continue to do things that make you happy while multiplying your happiness with your partner.

What do you really desire?

What is stopping you from living it?

Write it down

Chemical Imbalance

"Our body stores DNA from every chemistry it's ever received."

Due to these increasingly common chemical changes in people, there are more hospital visits. Especially when negative energy is generated, which is the worst way to treat the body, leading to stagnation or unproductive distractions. Chemical imbalances happen when:

A woman in her adolescence may have 5, 6, or 10 boyfriends, but has only been intimate with one in true love, earning respect from the others. The relationship did not work out, and they separated. Later, she meets her other half and gets married. That woman will never need a change of skin (chemistry).

A woman in her adolescence dates 5, 8, or 10 men and has relations with all of them; then she is considered "indecent," which means she is constantly undergoing changes of skin, or in other words, CHEMICAL CHANGES in her development.

Change of chemistries, rigid lingams, and aggression are what destroy development in adolescence; fundamentally, the change in chemistry is what causes a change in metabolism in the growing body and is part of its physical needs. If you are hungry and do not eat, you feel bad; if you are sleepy and don't sleep, you feel bad; if you have a physiological

need (like needing to use the bathroom and don't), you feel bad; and if you don't meet chemical needs (like skin changes), you feel bad.
chemical change as it got used to during puberty, it malfunctions and doesn't naturally create fluids or antibodies.

What can affect the body the most to affect its chemical imbalance is the reception of different fluids from different people in short periods of time. When the male ejaculates inside the woman, he is leaving his DNA in that woman, and vice versa. This is like a cream our bodies are absorbing. The longer that DNA stays inside of the body, the more the body absorbs its genes and takes them as its own. If it's repeated with one person, these genes will incrust even deeper.

This can be observed in the feline breed that during mating season, they have relations with multiple males and then produce kittens with a variety of colors and traits, as each male carries different genes from his birth.
happen in the human race, as we possess what is called intelligence and fidelity.

This is why sometimes there are kids that are born with different traits than the parents, because if there was any absorbed DNA inside of the woman prior to that birth, they have a possibility of having a genetic trait of that person. This is why condoms (preferably natural non-toxic) are so important and being sure of the person you are sleeping with is even more important. Of course, parents are made by who raises you, but when it comes to genetic diseases, all of this is important to know. If there is no trait of a genetic disease in your family or your partner's, and your kids have it, and at some point, in life, there was a deposit of sperm on the woman, then that is the possibility of absorption. I know this is very delicate information and there are already people making this public, we have always abstained from mentioning it publicly because it can cause rejection from parents to kids, which should never happen. What was done is done, and there is no going backwards. What's important is that this information gets to newer generations to prevent further harm. A parent is the person who raises the child, not only the one who provides the sperm, but it also doesn't make your offspring any less yours.

The fluids our body produces are not to be taken lightly. These fluids transfer everything that is in your DNA, your energy. If negative energy is being generated, then all the person's bad genes will pass along, but if positive energy is being generated and the giver is healthy, you can even receive the healing to your health issues. Our bodies are intelligent, and when they get used to one another, they will care for each other. The key is energy.

So, every time a woman is kissing, or worse, drinking or swallowing semen deposit, allowing it to touch her skin, this is acting as a cream that is being absorbed by the skin. It is why it's so important to take the time and get to know who you will be involved with and to generate positive energy always and have a healthier lineage.

When the body is going through a chemical imbalance, it will react with a smelly discharge both in men and women. The genitals are a flush system, and anything that does not belong to your body will be discharged through your fluids. When and if you notice color changes or odor, your body is cleansing itself. If it goes on for a while, you should get a closer examination. If nothing turns up, now at least you know why.

It's normal that cancerous nodules appear in women who had premature sexual encounters with different chemistry, meaning different partners. This is why it's important to do a monthly check up of the female conduit to make sure there isn't any pain or rigid zones that if are left alone, could become a real health problem. It is especially important to have finger penetration, and the more, the better, in both passages, vaginal and anal, because polyps form in both walls. Always check up and treat with the exercises. What these exercises do is scrape and heal. We massage every other part of our body; the pelvic area must not be a stranger as all our tendons pass through our pelvic zone.

Female Recovery

Women who experienced several sexual failures need recovery, and it all begins with the mind. Let's remember that for men, after a few months, it becomes a sexual chore rather than sexual pleasure when a woman has a shield and loss of sensitive spots, having to thrust for many minutes without achieving the woman's orgasm or pleasure, even more frustrating for men who reach an orgasm in a reasonable time. Women are left exposed to never experiencing an orgasm, and this leads to separation. There is recovery; where there is a will, there is a solution.

In 2022 it was proven by our team that after a woman has constant romantic failures, when a woman finds THE MAN, meaning the one who sets her on a new path and takes a new direction in her life where she truly and deeply falls in love with that man, she can revive and regenerate new sensitive spots, making her body react as a normal woman's again.

Clearly, to begin this journey, she must not have incorporated negativities in her body, no negative spheres that block the feeling. This means that before beginning a path of reawakening, the female has to go through negative energy purges. What's remarkable is that true love in feeling causes new sensitive points to flourish, making her feel complete again, feeling pleasure again in such that she doesn't even need penetration; even feeling the warmth of her partner's hand, conversation, closeness, can lead her to experience orgasms generated by her body constantly, such as when she was a virgin. Everything is driven by the energy of love when there is truly love.

If you are someone who has been with more than 1 sexual partner in your youth, you should consider these consequences; the more change of chemistry, the more reactions your body will have after 27 years of age and aggravating more after 35. So, if you happen to have hysteria, migraines, feel strange, lost, depressed, etc., now you know why. The only thing that can balance your body back to normal is to have a chemistry change.

If you are in a relationship, consent is everything, and picking someone that is positive is important; you will treat this encounter as a health need and nothing more. How often or how many times your body will need this depends on how many people you were with in your youth and how bad your symptoms are. But there is no need for pills when you can balance your hormones naturally.

I met a couple once, where the female was very promiscuous in her youth, and she was considered a nymph in her 50's. Her husband would accompany her to have sex with other men because he knew if she didn't, she would become hysterical, and that was the only way she felt happiness. He suffered, of course, but he knew it was for her health. This has been one of the roughest cases I have encountered, but without them knowing why they were doing what they were doing, they found a solution to her health issues. These cases can vary from something very simple to very difficult cases like that one.

So, if you are someone who has a mild reaction to your chemical imbalance, you might just need a once every couple of years exchange, and then you will feel normal again. This is very delicate information and I share it because I know for a lot of loving marriages that have found themselves against the wall not finding solutions, or wrongly fall into swinging which is not ideal, this information can heal their relationship, but the mind must be very certain of the intention behind the act so there is no confusion. If your mind is weak and you do not think you can handle it, it's better not to engage in this. Knowing your partner's past is extremely necessary to know what you will be facing in the future, to know if you are mentally prepared to deal with something like this.

The need for a change of skin (chemistry); this hormonal mismatch does not have an immediate solution, and this need cannot be ignored. The issue of chemical imbalance due to a wrongly adapted adolescent body must be understood between partners so that there is no corruption of love, because the lack of changing chemistries, generates nervousness and even aggression in the harmony of the couple, tolerance disappears, and the couple can become corrupted due to the lack of hormones generated by the change of chemistry (skin) necessity. With time, this need of change of chemistry will dissipate as the mind of the woman needs to be very aware and conscious of why and what is happening, acknowledging that a change of chemistry is only viable for health reasons and not to degenerate the purpose of the action into becoming a bad habit, leading her towards a wrong path again. So, if the woman has analyzed that she falls into the category of needing that change of chemistry, the couple will submit to the act of proving this for health and progress purposes only when hormonal imbalances happen, like hysteria, nervousness, lack of tolerance, etc. The mind must be determined that it's acting on a need and not feeding a desire. With time, the determination of the female mind will teach the body to no longer need a change of chemistry by re-adapting itself to only need its one and only partner. Determination and willingness in healing and belonging only to one person are what make this change possible.

The difference is that when there is love in the couple, and the sensitive points are opened, any need for chemical change or change of skin happens more quickly and with less frequency of need.

Awakening Sensitive Spots

Unfortunately, women are the ones who suffer from more sensitivity loss than men. Women are the carriers of life; therefore, they are meant to be as pure as possible, to be able to conceive a healthy offspring with a pure lineage.

The loss of sensitive spots is the cause of so many divorces today; it's important to acknowledge if this is something that you suffer from. To analyze your sensitive spots, you will begin from the top down, if you are with a partner, it will be easier as you can explore the entire body. From your head to the back of your ears, your neck and mouth, inside of your mouth, your tongue, your cheeks, a key point being your nipples, throughout your back, arms, stomach, and reaching the main area, which is your genitals. The most common sensitive spot to be lost in women is the nipples; they may go numb, especially if there has been a surgery. The worst thing women can do is get implants through their areola being cut; a large percentage of patients will lose their nipple sensitivity, not all, but a majority, these can be reawakened.

Using common sense, let's admit that anywhere in your body that your loved one touches should feel amazing since you are with the person you love, so just them being near you will be enough to have your energy and arousal levels activated. If this doesn't happen, it means you have a bit of a shield, and if you are alone, you can still explore which areas of your body are numb.

Let's dedicate some time to each area with lots of love and patience. It is the energy of love and caring that will wake up the body faster than anything else, but it can also be done with a partner who is conscious of what they are trying to help you achieve. It will take longer because you don't have the love energy, but it will still work eventually.

By reaching moments of arousal and only focusing on these dormant areas while there is an arousal in play, will slowly tell the body it needs to create new sensitive spots. When something is dormant, it needs to be treated with a little bit of pressure to awaken it. So, the breast area needs to be pressed, and the nipples pinched and pulled outwards. This will cause some discomfort at first, but it will help awaken the sensitivity back in the breasts with time. Areas like the neck need to be treated with kisses, same as the back, which can be tried with feathers or the soft touch of the hand.

To awaken the mouth, from the lips to the tongue and cheeks, there needs to be a lot of conscious kissing and oral practice. Some women do not like to do oral, and this is a perfect example to know their mouth's sensitive spots are not functioning. When the mouth has all its spots working, the arousal from doing oral sex to their partner will feel extremely arousing and will produce involuntary orgasms. The mouth and the yoni are connected, so activating one end activates the other.

The awakening of sensitive spots does not happen from one day to the next; it needs to be taken with patience and persistence. Yoni sensitive spots would fall into the exercise of the ring elasticity practice. Having a dormant spot means numbness or discomfort, so these practices will be uncomfortable at first until you finally start awakening new spots. It will make life all worth it. You need to reach high moments of pleasure with your full body, so that you can then experience a full-body energetic orgasm as often as possible. An energetic orgasm is when all your sensitive spots activate by themselves. This is achieved by both women and men. In men, it happens when the feeling of an orgasm happens, but they do not release fluid or sperm, other than the normal lubrication. This is what everyone should be experiencing daily. It is a constant current of electricity going through your body at different times of the day. A rush that travels through your body and makes you shiver. This is the real connection between you and the ether.

Working on generating energy in couples is an act of love, but for those who do not have love and do so by mutual agreement in pursuit of positive energy, it is done very slowly, with a pumping motion where the goal is pleasure and not vaginal destruction due to emotional release. It is something very delicate that makes the woman feel continuous pleasure. They can work for a long time, not just a few minutes, and the pleasure is prolonged. It is the woman who begins to need more rhythm or speed of movement or passive aggressiveness without destruction; she regulates it, not the man, and she asks for it to be faster.

So now you know. Your body is a living organism with thousands of electric spots that need to be in fully functioning condition. Reawaken your body from the inside out, use more hands, retain more energy, value your orgasms, and live in a constant arousal state. That is a life of pure pleasure, one left in very few towns in the world.

Using Energy for
Health, Wealth, & Love

Have you ever taken any self-help therapy? This is the chance to put that to work, but with active energy, which was what you were missing when you did all of those self-help therapies and never got anywhere.

We established that the ritual of generating energy activates all three points of energy: the voice, which acts like an amplifier, the mind, which is the thought guide, and the movement, which is the thruster. So why would you only try abundance meditation with meditation alone? Whatever you need will be put into the universe with the strength of whatever energy you give it. So, if your strongest energy generator is arousal and even more so, intimacy at all levels, then this would be the energy that you would be using to send your thoughts for abundance to the universe. All those actions, from a hug to a hold in intimacy, add up.

When you reach a level of 100% openness within your channel, this is when meditations like the law of attraction will work seamlessly without much generating sexually, because you will be channeling this energy daily. This is where you will manifest your dreams; every thought you have, and anything you think of, becomes a reality faster, if it is meant for you, of course. So, when you see a neighbor who seems to be doing everything right, they are

From the simple action of holding a hand or keeping them present in your mind. Your body creates that spark of energy just by those small things, and a perfect way of knowing this is because your body and chemistry will also release its reaction to that person.

These three points, unfortunately, can only be reached if you're in a relationship because, of course, you can have self-love, but it won't complete the unconditional love for another. You must have both energies to complete a full circle.

If you are yet without a partner, then focus on your goal of bettering yourself from the inside out, until you attract the right person for your better self, not for a broken self.

Energy Retention

Energy retention does not mean you are abstaining from generating arousal and sexual energy. It means you are using your body accordingly so that it has time to recover, regain, and provide when needed. For the male abstaining from releasing means he will channel energy for his partner, and when the time comes, he will deliver this positive energy he has channeled to his female partner, charging her, and she will then have the job of putting that energy to work. If you are not in a relationship, you will retain your energy for your own personal growth. You must listen to your body when it's time to let go. If you release constantly, you never allow your body to really recover, use, and accumulate this strength.

Retaining your life force is the best thing you could do, but there are ways, and it's not the same for everyone. If you are someone that lives on the beach daily, you are attending a place of healing daily where your energy is being transmuted by the ocean water. So, you can do energy retention with great benefit, also because you are charging from the sun. It all depends on your surroundings, nature, outdoors, and the sun.

If you are someone who has a stressful job and your household as well, you will be absorbing negativity daily. It is like when you walk on the street, and dust or dirt gets on you; you need to shower and cleanse; energy is the same process. Being exposed to hundreds of people a day means you are being exposed to their energy, which would mean that you are charging up with some negative energy daily, and since everyone has a different vibration, they inevitably shed it off wherever they go. Have you ever crossed paths with someone who all they know to say is what is wrong with their life? In these situations, which is most people, you would not benefit from retention all the time because you need to cleanse from excess negative energy. If you have positivity at home, that will balance and burn off any negative energy accumulated from work, but if you are not generating positive energy anywhere, the negative one you are absorbing will start making you feel heavy, dense, tired, lonely, depressed, and even sick. You need to cleanse yourself from this energy and the only way of doing so is through masturbation.

So, you can try retaining your energy for as long as you can and only act on a cleansing if you feel any of the above symptoms. The density of the release will be thick and pasty and mostly white; the thickness and pastiness are the key to knowing it's negative.

Your body will tell you when it's crucial to cleanse toxic energy.

When you start retaining your energy, you will feel an immense amount of strength, confidence, and arousal. You are holding on to your creative energy, to your battery life, and building it up increasingly. Learning to use it and releasing it only, when necessary, will bring interesting changes to your life. It is about getting a hold of your channel.

The problem happens when you adapt your body to emptying your energy every so often, some people daily, getting used to the addictive sense of an empty orgasm. When you release, you are emptying yourself, and if you do not have a positive source from where to charge back up, then you will always be in a stagnant situation. Your body will channel energy little by little to fulfill itself and use it towards your health, and by emptying it constantly you are barely saving any energy to stay healthy. See, the energy will recharge the body, and the more that fuel is inside, and we learn to move it and transmute it, the more benefit we can get from it and even learn to radiate it to others.

Energy needs to be mobilized through strong conscious breath work, so when you feel arousal, you can release so much pressure from the genitals and move it towards your brain, almost as if by pulling the energy upwards, you are feeding your brain with more power, even activating more neurons. Remember, we are energy, and our brain can be nourished from sparks of energy to feed the neurons, which will then command our channel to connect to higher frequencies and so on.

Retention does not mean you don't exercise your sexual energy. Remember, this is the energy you need to be activating at least once a day if you want to reach maximum strength, which means you are constantly activated throughout the day. The more you activate your arousal throughout the day, the more energy your body will generate, allowing it to store more energy inside, keeping it healthier. When you train your body to allow itself to feel freely throughout the day, and you reach that level of a constant arousal, you no longer will associate arousal with sex, but view it as a heightened state of consciousness, where you are connected to another dimension where everything is beautiful, peaceful and loving. That parallel universe some have the chance of seeing, and once you see it, you will never be or act the same.

If you have trouble doing this, do not do it all at once and just slow down on your releases every time a little longer until you can go about your months in a different state of arousal. See, instead of releasing the feeling you love so much, you are going to hold on to it throughout the day and night. Can you imagine what happens inside your body when you start to store that amount of energy?

Your cells start regenerating, your body warms up, works better, your mind will be focused and clear, and best of all, you will be accumulating more energy for help in external situations that have nothing to do with your body. You will start to radiate this energy out to others, this feeling of pleasure that lives inside of you, and you are holding on to as a natural state of existence. Could you imagine how your mind will feel in a longer state of arousal? Where you do not feel urges, anxiety, stress...The world would be a world of joy and peace, a pleasurable state of existence.

The longer you may go with retaining your energy, the larger your channel of energy will become, because it will learn each time to store more amounts of energy, meaning you can also last longer in a sexual encounter, feeling pleasure for longer amounts of time. You should never retain something that comes naturally; your body needs to have freedom of expression. If you retain for a few months and you are accumulating negativity, you will feel denser. It's not bad to release when you are training retention; it's just important to do so when your body absolutely needs it, to cleanse toxic energy.

It doesn't make you weak; it's using the act for what it's intended for. Once you cleanse your body from toxic energy, it will replenish again, and you will notice that each time you can go longer without releasing. If I had to give you a time of retention that would be healthy for you, it would be around 3 months. Clear your energy every 3 months if you are single, if you are in a relationship, go as long as you want because regardless of it you will recharge. A relationship will benefit more from energy work when the male stores enough power to then give to the woman, and this should be given orally so the female body recharges. If the man is positive and pure of toxic energy, he will store energy to give to the woman when needed. If the man or woman has a stressful job and needs release, they will aid each other's needs.

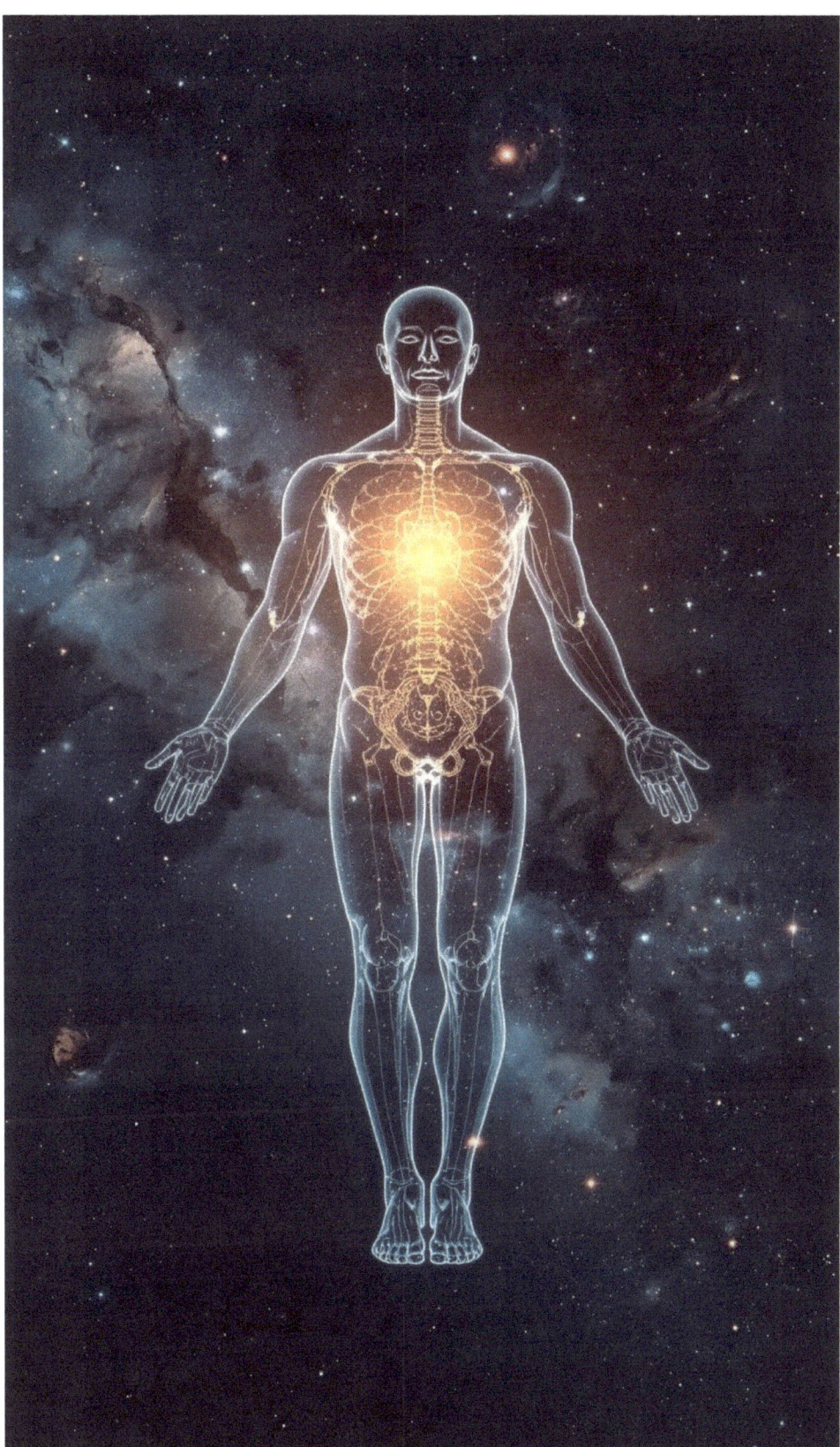

Love vs Lust

There is no sexual act that is negative as long as it's done with positive energy. This means that even the acts that you might see as a bit perverted (staying within the normal acts, no pain) will always generate positive energy if you are acting out of love. This means even two strangers can come together with a conscious thought of generating energy, and not having sex and the energy would be positive.

The difference between lust and love is that lust is a carnal feeling we get directly in our groin, and love is a butterfly feeling we get on a more spiritual level. One will leave you drained from positivity, and one will fill you with progress. One will heighten you, the other will dim you. These are the differences between sex and generating positive energy.

You can generate positive sexual energy with a partner that is not your partner officially. Keep in mind to just use your hands and mouth and not consume each other's fluids in preference. If the intention of both participants is to create energy, practice, and heighten their channel, then they will not generate negativity because there are pure intentions involved. Moving energy and maintaining elasticity are necessary when done with a conscience.

After all of this information, it's now time for you to compile what you think you can make use of and, most importantly, share that knowledge with future generations so we can foster better and healthier futures and a world where positivity reigns.

Perseverance

There isn't anything you can do in this life and be constantly successful at it without perseverance. What differs some people from others is the will to move on. How much fuel do you have inside to power a dream? This is, of course, energy.

Impossible doesn't exist, everything has a way, and if you haven't found it yet, it's simply because it's not for you yet; keep persevering in what you truly desire and what sparks up your soul. When there are obstacles on the way, it's simply a way of proving your worthiness of what you believe you deserve. We believe we deserve everything, yet the only way to make our wishes a reality is by creating the energy we need to make them a manifestation. The higher the energy generation, the higher the manifestation. The mind is not enough when the channel is corrupt or not generating proper energy.

Use the content in this book to better master your channel and with time, be rewarded by something that has no price: fulfillment of life itself, where your existence is enough to be a constant flow of positive energy for you, your family and the world. I won't wish you good luck, but a good journey on a new illuminated path with the proper information to build your own success.

THE END

www.ingramcontent.com/pod-product-compliance
Lightning Source LLC
Chambersburg PA
CBHW071315150426
43191CB00007B/636